Proposing Empirical Research

A Guide to the Fundamentals

Fourth Edition

Mildred L. Patten

 Pyrczak Publishing

P.O. Box 250430 • Glendale, CA 91225

"Pyrczak Publishing" is an imprint of Fred Pyrczak, Publisher, A California Corporation.

Although the author and publisher have made every effort to ensure the accuracy and completeness of information contained in this book, we assume no responsibility for errors, inaccuracies, omissions, or any inconsistency herein. Any slights of people, places, or organizations are unintentional.

Project Director: Monica Lopez

Editorial assistance provided by Cheryl Alcorn, Randall R. Bruce, Jenifer Dill, Brenda Koplin, Hank Rudisill, Erica Simmons, Mel Yiasemide, and Sharon Young.

Cover design by Robert Kibler and Larry Nichols.

Printed in the United States of America by Malloy, Inc.

ISBN 1-884585-89-2

Contents

Continued →

Notes

Introduction to the Fourth Edition

This book was written for students writing their first proposals for empirical research. Some students will be doing this as part of a culminating undergraduate course such as a senior research seminar. Others will be required to write a research proposal as a class project at the graduate level. Still others will have their first experience when they are required to prepare a proposal for their thesis or dissertation research. Ideally, such students should have taken at least one course in research methods and statistics, or should be taking such courses concurrently while using this book.

It is also assumed that students using this book are already familiar with the process of searching for academic literature. Appendices A and B are included at the end of this book for students who need to review the methods for locating literature and related statistics electronically.

Organization

Part A of this book is designed to help students select a problem area and develop tentative research questions, purposes, and hypotheses.

In Part B, students are encouraged to reevaluate and refine their research questions, purposes, and hypotheses in light of the literature on their topics, relevant theories, and the feasibility of executing their research ideas.

In Part C, students are reminded of the major approaches to research (i.e., types of research) and are encouraged to select a suitable type. Sometimes the type of research selected (e.g., qualitative) has implications for how research purposes, questions, and hypotheses are conceptualized and stated. Hence, some students will want to refine their research ideas further after considering the material in this part.

In Part D, students are shown how to organize and evaluate the literature they have collected in anticipation of the writing process.

The remaining parts of this book present guidelines for writing various components of a standard research proposal. Throughout these chapters, students will find short examples that illustrate important writing techniques.

Model Proposals

Nine model proposals are included near the end of this book. They are *not* presented as "ideal" proposals because a proposal that is a model of excellence for one purpose (e.g., as a project for a senior undergraduate seminar) may fall far short for another purpose (e.g., seeking major funding for research from a government agency). Instead, they are presented as examples of solid proposals that are consistent with the major recommendations in this book. Students and instructors may react to the proposals in classroom discussions. For example, instructors may wish to point out which parts of a sample proposal are written in a manner suitable for the specific purpose of a student's proposal and which parts need more (or less) explication and detail.

Benefits of Writing a Solid Proposal

Of course, a solid, well-formulated proposal is needed in order to secure approval for the proposed research. In addition, a proposal serves as an informal contract because those who approve the proposal are agreeing that if the research is executed as planned, the research will be approved when presented in a research report, thesis, or dissertation. To avoid misunderstandings, this "contract," like all others, should be as explicit and specific as possible—even if the proposed research is exploratory. Finally, a solid research proposal can serve as the framework for writing the final research report. For example, if a full-fledged literature review is written for the proposal, it might be used as the literature review in the research report.

Cautionary Notes

Students writing a proposal under the supervision of an instructor should seek feedback throughout the process, especially while selecting a research problem and formulating research purposes, questions, or hypotheses. Writing a complete proposal without such feedback could result in rejection of the entire work.

It is important to note that this book presents a framework and guidelines for preparing a standard research proposal as envisioned by this author. As with evaluation of any type of writing, there may be legitimate differences of opinion. Students should defer to their instructors when this occurs.

About the Fourth Edition

The major change from the Third Edition to the Fourth Edition is the inclusion of three new model proposals: Proposals 1, 4, and 8. Of special note is Proposal 4, which is for single-subject research, a type of research not covered in earlier editions. Also, a new topic on preparing a reference list (Topic 49) has been added.

Readers with suggestions for changes or additions to future editions may write to me in care of the publisher at the address on the title page or by sending comments to me via e-mail at Info@Pyrczak.com.

Mildred L. Patten

Part A

Getting Started

In this part of the book, you will learn how to identify and evaluate broad problem areas in which you might want to conduct research. In addition, you will learn how to *combine* variables of different types to form research questions, purposes, and hypotheses.

While some of the exercises in this part ask you to practice writing research questions, purposes, and hypotheses, you are strongly urged to avoid making a final selection for your research proposal until you have also completed Part B of this book, which will help you evaluate your tentative ideas for research. To use an analogy, *do not marry yourself* to an idea. *Date* several ideas, get to know them well, check out their families, and consider their future prospects. Part B will help you with these activities.

Notes

Topic 1

What Is Empirical Research?

The term *empiricism* refers to making *observations* to obtain knowledge. In everyday life, we all make informal observations of the people and things around us, and very often, we use these observations as a basis for making decisions. For example, a teacher might observe that his or her students seem bored and decide to switch to a livelier instructional activity.

The term *empirical research* refers to making *planned* observations. By following careful plans for making observations, we engage in a systematic, thoughtful process that deserves to be called *research*.

First, we need to plan *what to observe*. For example, we might wish to observe boredom in the classroom. What other variables should we plan to observe in order to aid our understanding of boredom? Maybe we should consider skill areas, such as math versus creative drawing. Maybe we should consider teaching styles or the match between each student's abilities and the instructional materials that are assigned to him or her. The possibilities are almost endless, so a researcher needs to select the variables that seem most promising.

Second, we need to plan *whom to observe*. For example, to study boredom in the classroom, we would plan what types of students to observe (e.g., elementary and/or secondary, middle-class and/or lower-socioeconomic-status students, and so on).

Third, we need to plan *how to observe*. How will we measure boredom (as well as other variables that might be related to boredom)? Should we ask students directly if they are bored using a questionnaire? By interviewing them? Should we observe the expressions on their faces and infer whether students are bored? If so, who will make the observations, and on what basis will they make the inferences (i.e., what types of facial expressions will be counted as indicating boredom)?

Next, we need to plan *when to observe*. Observations made on a hot Friday afternoon might yield very different results from those made on a clear spring morning.

Finally, we should *plan how to analyze the data* and interpret them. Will we calculate the percentage of students who appear bored while participating in cooperative group activities versus how many appear bored when working individually on worksheets? Will we try to correlate boredom with other variables such as socioeconomic status?

In this book, you will learn how to write a formal research proposal in which all these elements are addressed.

Exercise for Topic 1

Directions: If you already have some ideas for empirical research projects, briefly describe them below. If possible, describe two or more (using additional space if necessary). The ideas you write here will give you talking points for classroom discussions and should be thought of as only tentative. As you work through this book, you will probably decide to greatly modify or even abandon your responses to this exercise in favor of more suitable ones.

First Set of Ideas:

1. *What* might you observe?

   The main variable (e.g., boredom in the classroom) is:

   Other variables (e.g., teaching styles) are:

2. *Whom* might you observe?

3. *How* might you observe your main variable (e.g., a test, an interview)?

4. *When* might you make the observations?

Second Set of Ideas:

1. *What* might you observe?

   The main variable (e.g., boredom in the classroom) is:

   Other variables (e.g., teaching styles) are:

2. *Whom* might you observe?

3. *How* might you observe your main variable (e.g., a test, an interview)?

4. *When* might you make the observations?

Topic 2

Identifying Broad Problem Areas

Most beginning students should identify two or three broad problem areas in which they might wish to conduct research. These are broad areas in which many different types of specific research projects may be undertaken. Examples that illustrate what is meant by *broad problem areas* include the following:

- Attitudes toward mathematics
- Alcohol abuse
- Homelessness

Among the sources of ideas for broad problem areas are textbooks that were used in previous courses. Often, the authors of textbooks point out areas in which there is controversy or areas that are not fully fleshed out. For example, in the first chapter of his textbook on educational and psychological measurement, Thorndike[1] identifies "some current issues in measurement," which include "testing minority individuals" and "invasion of privacy." In a later chapter, he discusses "current and emerging issues" in the assessment of exceptional children. In yet another chapter, he discusses "problems with personality and interest measures." In each of these sections, the textbook author identifies several broad areas in need of additional research.

Other sources that may help in the identification of a broad problem area for research include the following:

- Lecture notes from previous courses.
- Review and reference publications such as the *Encyclopedia of Educational Research*, which contains 2,701 articles organized under 16 broad headings.[2] The articles cover diverse areas such as AIDS education, education of pregnant and parenting teenagers, and athletics in higher education.
- "Signature" publications of major professional associations, such as *American Psychologist*, published by the American Psychological Association, which carries articles of broad interest to psychologists (as opposed to research journals that carry reports on narrowly defined research).
- Journals that specialize in reviews of research, such as *Psychological Bulletin*. Typically, these reviews provide a synthesis of research in a variety of problem areas.
- Discussions with professors, especially those who might be serving on your thesis or dissertation committee.
- Discussions with employers and colleagues.

In Topic 3, we will consider how to evaluate problem areas you are considering.

---

[1] Thorndike, R. M. (1997). *Measurement and evaluation in psychology and education* (6th ed.). Columbus, OH: Merrill.

[2] Most academic fields have encyclopedias, dictionaries, and/or handbooks that summarize research in broad areas. Consult your reference librarian to see if these are available in your discipline.

Exercise for Topic 2

Directions: List three broad problem areas in which you might be interested in conducting research. For each, indicate what brought the area to your attention (e.g., textbooks, personal experience, suggestions from others) and rate the degree of your interest in the area on a scale from 1 to 5.

First Problem Area:

1. What brought this area to your attention?

2. How interested are you in this area?

               Very interested   5   4   3   2   1   Not at all interested

Second Problem Area:

1. What brought this area to your attention?

2. How interested are you in this area?

               Very interested   5   4   3   2   1   Not at all interested

Third Problem Area:

1. What brought this area to your attention?

2. How interested are you in this area?

               Very interested   5   4   3   2   1   Not at all interested

Topic 3
Evaluating Broad Problem Areas

Each of the broad problem areas you identified in the exercise for Topic 2 should now be evaluated. Get feedback from professors, other students, and colleagues. If you are proposing research for a thesis or dissertation, you will want to very carefully consider the interests of the professors who might serve on your committee. If you fail to follow this advice, you might become an "orphan" with no one especially interested in giving you that extra measure of help you will inevitably need at some point in your work.[1]

Other important criteria for evaluating a broad problem area include:

1. Is the problem area in the mainstream of your field of study?

    Beginners should consider working in the mainstream because they normally have better academic backgrounds on mainstream issues. Also, it is easier to locate faculty and other students to help with research on mainstream issues. For example, the broad problem area of "homelessness" is more of a mainstream issue for a social work major than for a nursing major—although individuals in both professions work with the homeless.

2. Is there a substantial body of literature on the problem area?[2]

    At first, you might be tempted to think that an area with a substantial body of literature is probably one in which researchers have exhausted most of the interesting research possibilities. However, the reverse is almost always true: As an area becomes better researched, new and *more interesting* facets often emerge. As one researcher builds on the research of another, complex layers of information and data that reveal its complexity become available— suggesting additional promising lines of research.

3. Is the problem area timely?

    Timely issues are more likely to be of interest to potential readers of your research. In addition, conducting research on them is more likely to advance your career and lead to funding opportunities for your research. Try to distinguish between timely areas (on which there typically will be at least some published research) and merely fashionable areas that will fade when tomorrow's newspaper headlines are different from today's.

---

[1] When you approach professors with a broad problem area, some of them might want to dive into the thick of things and ask you for your specific research purposes or hypotheses. If this happens, explain that you are not at that stage yet—that you are considering broad areas and trying to identify faculty who might be interested in working with you.

[2] At this point in your academic career, you probably know how to search the major computerized databases of literature in your academic area. For those who do not, Appendix A describes the basics of this process.

Exercise for Topic 3

Directions: Rewrite the names of the three broad problem areas you identified in the exercise for Topic 2. Then briefly evaluate each one.

First Problem Area:

1. Is the problem area in the mainstream of your field of study? Explain.

2. Is there a substantial body of literature on the problem area? Explain.

3. Is the problem area timely? Explain.

Second Problem Area:

1. Is the problem area in the mainstream of your field of study? Explain.

2. Is there a substantial body of literature on the problem area? Explain.

3. Is the problem area timely? Explain.

Third Problem Area:

1. Is the problem area in the mainstream of your field of study? Explain.

2. Is there a substantial body of literature on the problem area? Explain.

3. Is the problem area timely? Explain.

Topic 4

Identifying and Combining Variables

To narrow a broad problem area down to a specific research topic, it is helpful to brainstorm a list of *variables* within the area that might be of interest. Most variables can be thought of as belonging to one of three families:

1. *Knowledge*

Research often focuses on what people know about some topic. Examples of knowledge variables include:

- Knowledge of how HIV is transmitted (Note that people will differ, or *vary*, in the amount of this knowledge. Hence, it is called a *variable*.)
- Knowledge of community resources for people with HIV
- Knowledge of treatment options for HIV

2. *Opinions and Feelings*

Considerable research deals with this family of variables. Examples include:

- Attitudes toward people with HIV
- Opinions on federal support for research on HIV
- Depression among people with children who are HIV positive

3. *Overt Behavior/Action*

What people do is also of considerable interest. Examples of variables in this family include:

- Whether people flee when someone sitting next to them identifies him- or herself as HIV positive
- How much people donate to charities that assist individuals with HIV
- Use of free clinics by people who are HIV positive

We can combine variables to form interesting research questions. Using two of the *opinions and feelings variables* mentioned earlier, we could ask

- Do those with more favorable attitudes toward people with HIV favor more federal support for research on HIV than those with less favorable attitudes?

We can also combine variables across two *different* families of variables and ask research questions such as

- Do people with more knowledge of how HIV is transmitted have more favorable attitudes toward people with HIV than those with less knowledge?

The exercise for this topic will ask you to brainstorm some variables from each of the three families and try combining them—but do not fall in love yet, and do not marry yourself to a research question! There is still quite a bit of work to do before making a commitment.

Exercise for Topic 4

Directions: Complete this exercise using one of the broad problem areas you named in your responses to the exercise for Topic 3. If you are still considering more than one, use additional space to complete this exercise for each additional area.

Name a broad problem area here:

1. List at least four *knowledge* variables within the problem area.

2. List at least four *opinions and feelings* variables within the problem area.

3. List at least four *overt behavior/action* variables within the problem area.

4. Combine two variables from *one family of variables* into a research question.

5. Combine two variables from *two different families of variables* into a research question.

Topic 5
Identifying Treatment Variables

When researchers give treatments such as an aspirin a day to one group and a placebo to another, they create a variable known as an *independent variable*. The people in the study *vary* (or differ) because of what the researcher has done to them. (Those in one group have thinner blood than those in the other because of the blood-thinning effects of aspirin.) The formal name of a study in which a researcher gives treatments is an *experiment*.

As you plan your research, you will need to decide whether you wish to conduct an experiment. To make this decision, consider possible treatments you might give to affect the variables you named in your responses to Questions 1 through 3 in the exercise for Topic 4. In other words, consider what treatments you might give to affect *knowledge*, or the *opinions and feelings*, or the *overt behavior/action* of potential participants in your research.

At first, some students think that conducting an experiment is inherently more difficult than conducting a nonexperimental study. However, the research literature is full of simple, revealing experimental studies. For example:

A researcher prepared two versions of a résumé. The two were identical except that one version stated "Health condition: Perfect" and the other stated "Health condition: Impaired vision." Different versions were mailed to different potential employers, and the number of positive responses from employers was counted.

As you can see, the potential employers were "treated" with different versions of the résumé. Note that the effort to conduct the experiment was not greater than the effort it would take to conduct an opinion survey by mail.

As you consider potential treatments, look for ones that might produce a big bang—that is, those that have a good chance of being highly effective. For example, tutoring children in math (the treatment) for a few hours would be unlikely to produce much of an effect on a nationally standardized math test. However, a few hours of tutoring on the addition of simple fractions might produce a big gain on a test that measures only this particular math skill. Of course, it is sometimes hard to guess in advance if a particular treatment will produce a big effect.

Although the exercise for this topic will ask you to identify some potential independent variables, note that you should immerse yourself in the literature on the topic that you eventually select to identify which treatments have already been tried and how effective they have been before making a final selection. Often, it is fruitful to try a modification of a treatment that was used in published research in order to see if the modified

11

treatment is more or less effective than the original one.

Note that an independent variable can have more than two types of treatments. For instance, a researcher might administer three types of counseling for reducing anxiety.

Exercise for Topic 5

PART A: Directions: This exercise is for practice only. If you will be conducting an experiment, you will want to explore the research literature carefully to identify promising treatments.

1. Select one of the *knowledge* variables that you listed in response to Question 1 in the exercise for Topic 4 and write it here:

   Name an *independent variable* (i.e., treatments) that might increase the knowledge.

2. Select one of the *opinions and feelings* variables that you listed in response to Question 2 in the exercise for Topic 4 and write it here:

   Name an *independent variable* (i.e., treatments) that might change the opinions and feelings.

3. Select one of the *overt behavior/action* variables that you listed in response to Question 3 in the exercise for Topic 4 and write it here:

   Name an *independent variable* (i.e., treatments) that might change the overt behavior/action.

PART B: Directions: On the following scale, rate how interested you are in conducting an experiment at this point in your planning. Explain the reason for your rating.

Very interested   5   4   3   2   1   Not at all interested

Topic 6
Considering Demographic Variables

Demographic variables are background characteristics of the participants you will be studying. Many demographics are considered in research in the social and behavioral sciences. Examples include:

- Highest (or current) educational level
- Socioeconomic status
- Age
- Major in school
- Employment status
- Gender

You should consider demographics at this point in planning your research because there probably will be some that you will want to *hold constant* in the study you are planning. For example, you might want to hold gender and educational level constant by studying only women enrolled in college. If so, you will probably want to add this information to your emerging research questions because it will be an important restriction on what you will be studying. For instance, this question might be posed:

- Among female college students, do those who have traveled abroad have more knowledge of world geography than those who have not traveled abroad?

Notice the three elements in the question: (1) two demographic variables (gender and educational level) that are held constant, (2) an overt behavior/action variable (traveling abroad), and (3) a knowledge variable.

There are three important considerations in identifying demographic variables to hold constant. First, there is the practical matter of the types of individuals to whom you have access. For example, if you teach fifth-grade students, you may wish to confine yourself to this readily available sample. Second, you should consider the demographic types that are most likely to exhibit the behaviors you wish to observe. For example, for a study on stress created by ageism, older adults are more likely to have had relevant experiences than younger adults. Third, you should consider whether holding a demographic variable constant will help to simplify your study so that it is manageable. For example, a study on AIDS prevention using only males or only females is inherently simpler than one with both males and females.

Note that important demographic variables that you do *not* hold constant will need to be described in your research report. For example, you may study college-level women who vary in age. You will want to plan to collect information on age so that you can describe this demographic characteristic in your research report. This can easily be done by reporting the percentage in each of several age categories or by reporting the average age of the participants in the research.

Exercise for Topic 6

Directions: Keep in mind that your responses to this exercise are for practice only. Final selection of one or more research questions should take place only after you complete Part B of this book.

1. Rewrite the research question that you wrote for Question 4 in the exercise for Topic 4 here:

   Revise the research question to include reference to one or more demographic variables that might be held constant (e.g., "Among female college students...").

2. Rewrite the research question that you wrote for Question 5 in the exercise for Topic 4 here:

   Revise the research question to include reference to one or more demographic variables that might be held constant (e.g., "Among female college students...").

Topic 7

Writing Purposes and Hypotheses

In Topics 4 through 6, you saw how variables can be combined to form *research questions*. Consider the following example of a research question with two variables (free-floating anxiety and success in quitting smoking) plus a demographic variable (age/adulthood) that is held constant.

- Among adults, is there a relationship between free-floating anxiety and success in quitting smoking?

Often, researchers prefer to state a *research purpose* (a statement instead of a question). Using the same variables as in the previous example, here is a research purpose:

- The purpose is to explore the relationship between free-floating anxiety and success in quitting smoking.

The choice between stating a research question and stating a research purpose is largely a matter of personal preference. However, notice that neither one predicts the outcome of the study. This is not true of hypotheses, which are considered next.

If you are willing to predict the nature of the relationship, you should state a *hypothesis* instead of a research question or purpose because a hypothesis indicates what you *expect* to find. Using the same variables as in the previous two examples, here is a research hypothesis:

- Adults who have more free-floating anxiety will be less successful in their

attempts to quit smoking than those with less anxiety.

While research questions, purposes, and hypotheses should be reasonably specific, avoid being overly specific about the anticipated statistical outcome. Here is one that is too specific:

- Adults who have more free-floating anxiety will be 55% less successful in quitting smoking than those with less anxiety.

It will be almost impossible for the data to support this hypothesis because there will have to be exactly 55% less (not 54%, not 56%, in fact, not any other percentage) for confirmation of the hypothesis. Thus, the hypothesis that says simply that there will be *less success* without quantification is a superior hypothesis.

As you consider possible research questions, purposes, and hypotheses, keep in mind that a research proposal may be based on more than one of them. Generally, however, they should be closely related. Here is an example in which there are three related hypotheses:

- Among adults, there is an inverse relationship between success in quitting smoking and
  1. free-floating anxiety,
  2. depression, and
  3. interpersonal dependency needs.

Exercise for Topic 7

Directions: You should still consider your responses to the following questions highly tentative. Final selection of research questions, purposes, and hypotheses should not be made until you have read Part B of this book.

1. Rewrite the research question that you wrote for Question 4 in the exercise for Topic 4 here:

   Revise the research question so that it is in the form of a *research purpose*:

   Revise the research question so that it is in the form of a *research hypothesis*:

2. Rewrite the research question that you wrote for Question 5 in the exercise for Topic 4 here:

   Revise the research question so that it is in the form of a *research purpose*:

   Revise the research question so that it is in the form of a *research hypothesis*:

Part B

A Closer Look at Problem Selection

Having completed Part A of this book, you should have several tentative research questions, purposes, or hypotheses within one or two broad problem areas. In this part, you will be encouraged to consider other possibilities within the problem areas, evaluate them, and make a final selection for your research proposal.

Note that the research questions, purposes, or hypotheses are the *heart* of your proposal. If they are not solid and suitable, your proposal will be unsatisfactory regardless of your excellence in writing the other portions of the proposal.

Notes

Finding Ideas in the Literature

Before making a final selection of research questions, purposes, or hypotheses on which to base your proposal, you should read extensively on the problem area(s) that you have selected. While reading books (especially textbooks) will give you a broad overview, at this point you need to immerse yourself in the specifics of how others have conducted research. These specifics can be found in reports of original research published in academic journals. Such reports (called *research articles*) can be identified electronically. See Appendix A if you are unfamiliar with conducting such searches. Although electronic databases often provide abstracts (summaries) of the articles, it is essential that you obtain copies of the full articles and carefully read them in their entirety.

As you read, pay special attention to *the specific research questions, purposes, or hypotheses* stated in the article. Usually, these can be found in the paragraph immediately above the heading "Method" in an article.

- Are the questions, purposes, or hypotheses similar to ones you have been considering for your research?
- Could any of them be modified to create a new problem that you might want to investigate?
- Were any of them sufficiently important that a replication of the study is warranted? Would you want to propose a replication (i.e., another study

designed to see if similar results are obtained)? Can you get approval from your instructor to propose a replication? (Note that for a learning exercise, your instructor may want you to propose original research rather than a replication.)

You should also pay special attention to the *discussion* sections that appear at the end of most research articles. In these discussions, researchers often describe the *limitations* (i.e., weaknesses) of their studies. Ask yourself whether you could propose research without these limitations. If so, you may want to propose a *modified replication* of a study in which you improve on the research methodology.

In their discussions, researchers also often describe *possible directions for future research*. Consider whether any are of sufficient interest to you that you might want to propose research along the lines suggested. These suggestions deserve careful consideration because they are being made by experienced researchers who have conducted publishable research on a topic within your problem area. Contrary to what some beginning students think, most researchers are more than happy to share their best research ideas with others. There is no greater compliment than having others build on one's completed research and having the original research cited as the inspiration.

Exercise for Topic 8

Directions: Read at least three reports of original research (research articles) in one of your problem areas, and answer the following questions.

1. Did the articles help you to refine the research questions, purposes, or hypotheses that you have been considering? Explain.

2. Did the articles give you ideas for new research questions, purposes, or hypotheses? Explain.

3. What other benefits, if any, did you get from reading the articles?

4. Do you believe that you are closer to making a final selection of research questions, purposes, or hypotheses to propose as a result of reading the journal articles? Explain.

Topic 9

Considering a Body of Literature

Before making a final selection of research questions, purposes, or hypotheses on which to base your proposal, you should consider the body of literature as a whole. In other words, read all the articles you have collected on your general topic and reflect on them *as a group*. Ask yourself the following questions:

- What are the trends in research perspectives *over time*? For instance, does newer research use conceptualizations different from older research? As a general rule, you will want to use the newer conceptualizations unless you have a very good reason for doing otherwise.

- Are there particular lines of research that have been especially fruitful in uncovering important results? Are there unfruitful lines that you will want to avoid?

- Are certain previous studies repeatedly cited by current researchers? If so, this may point you to the historical roots of current lines of research. You will want to read carefully such landmark or classic studies for possible ideas for your proposed research.

- Are there obvious gaps in the body of research literature? For example, have all the researchers used only college women as participants? Do you have access to other groups of women that you might propose to study?

Often, those who write research articles will help you to answer these questions. In Example 1, the researchers point out an important gap in a body of literature.

Example 1
Because most of the published research on prevention of youth substance use and abuse has been conducted with majority populations (i.e., white youth from the middle class), the question has been raised about whether interventions found to be effective with the majority group can be successful in preventing substance use and abuse among minority youth. With regard to that question, the limited amount of relevant empirical research has yielded mixed findings....[1]

In Example 2, the researchers point out what has been established as well as current trends, which might be considered as a topic for research.

Example 2
A vast literature now exists linking social support to well-being. Epidemiological studies show that people who have more supportive ties are less likely to become ill and more likely to live longer.... More recently, researchers who are interested in the effects that social relationships have on health have turned their attention to the negative side of social interactions [e.g., the effects of negative social interactions]....[2]

---

[1] Spoth, R., Guyll, M., Chao, W., & Molgaard, V. (2003). Exploratory study of a preventive intervention with general population African American families. *Journal of Early Adolescence, 23,* 435–468.

[2] Helgeson, V. S., Novak, S. A., Lepore, S. J., & Eton, D. T. (2004). Spouse social control efforts: Relations to health behavior and well-being among men with prostate cancer. *Journal of Social and Personal Relationships, 21,* 53–68.

Exercise for Topic 9

Directions: After considering the body of research in your problem area, answer the following questions.

1. Are there changes in the trends in research perspectives over time? Explain. If yes, how will they affect your formulation of research questions, purposes, or hypotheses?

2. Are there lines of research within your area that have been particularly fruitful? Unfruitful?

3. Are certain previous studies repeatedly cited in current research? If yes, have you read these landmark studies? Explain.

4. Have you found any obvious gaps in the research on your topic? Explain. If yes, will you consider proposing research to fill one or more of the gaps? Explain.

Topic 10

Considering Theories

A *theory* is a unified explanation for discrete observations that might otherwise be viewed as unrelated or contradictory. For instance, some tenets of expectancy theory are described in this example:

Example

> The basic tenet of expectancy theory suggests that individuals behave in ways that are self-serving.... According to the theory, the motivation to behave in certain ways is influenced by three factors. First is "instrumentality," which refers to the belief that change in behavior will result in self-serving outcomes. The stronger the belief, the more likely the behavior will change. Second is "valance," which refers to the value placed on the outcome. The more valued the outcome, the more likely it is that behavior will change. Third is "expectancy," which refers to the belief that exerting effort will lead to change.[1]

This theory has many implications for the study of the motivation to change. For instance, a stop-smoking program that helps clients to change their instrumentality, valance, *and* expectancy should be more effective than programs that involve only one or two of the factors. Such a prediction could be the basis of an experiment in which two or more types of stop-smoking programs are devised and tested.

Note that being able to say in a proposal that the research either will test some aspect of an important theory or has its origins in such a theory is usually an excellent way to help justify proposed research. This is true because the results are less likely to be viewed as isolated data. Instead, they are likely to contribute to understanding behavior in a larger context. Thus, you will want to consider whether your research questions, purposes, or hypotheses can be related to one or more theories.

Survey textbooks in most content areas usually cover only the most important, well-established theories. However, research on newer theories that are not as established may be more interesting and make more substantial contributions. As you read research articles in your problem area, you are likely to identify such theories. In addition, you might conduct an electronic database search in which you include the term *theory*. For example, a search of *PsycINFO*, the major database in psychology, using the terms "television," "violence," *and* "theory," identified 49 research articles, including one that explored the "tainted fruit theory," which leads to the prediction that "warning labels will increase interest in violent programs." Of course, those who conduct future research in this area might want to take account of this theory.[2]

Here is another example: Searching for "drug abuse" from 1996 to the present yielded 7,184 articles. Searching for

[1] Based on Casper, W. J., Fox, K. E., Sitzmann, T. M., & Landy, A. L. (2004). Supervisor referrals to work–family programs. *Journal of Occupational Health Psychology, 9*, 136–151.

[2] Bushman, B. J., & Stack, A. D. (1996). Forbidden fruit versus tainted fruit: Effects of warning labels on attraction to television violence. *Journal of Experimental Psychology: Applied, 2*, 207–226.

"drug abuse" *and* "theory" yielded a more manageable 354 articles. Restricting the search by specifying that "theory" must appear in the *titles* of the articles identified an even more manageable 49 articles. Note that the word "theory" in the title of an article suggests that the article emphasizes one or more underlying theories in the conceptualization of the research. These would be good articles to examine if a researcher wanted to relate his or her research to current theories.

Exercise for Topic 10

Directions: Consider the problem area that you believe you are most likely to pursue in your proposal.

1. In what problem area are you planning to conduct research?

2. Are you aware of any theories that might help you in planning your research?

3. Have you conducted an electronic database search using the term "theory"? If yes, what were the results? How helpful were the articles you identified by doing this?

Determining Feasibility

At this point, you should consider making a final selection of a problem area within which to propose research. You should also have a list of variables of interest within the area. The variables should have been derived from your study of research articles, including those with strong theoretical underpinnings. Also, you should combine variables into research questions. You should try to write a number of combinations so that you can evaluate them and choose the best among them.

For example, suppose that your original broad problem area was "homelessness," and you narrowed it to "the origins of homelessness." Some of the variables you might consider are drug abuse, mental retardation, child abuse, strength of family ties, and so on. Some research questions you might ask include:

- Do homeless adults tend to have a stronger history of drug abuse than comparable people who are not homeless?

- Are the children of homeless parents more likely to become homeless adults than are children of housed parents?

- To what factors do the "new" homeless (i.e., those who have been homeless for less than a year) attribute their homelessness?

As you know from Topic 7, you can rephrase a research *question* as a research *purpose*:

- The purpose is to identify the factors to which the "new" homeless attribute their homelessness.

Whether you use a *question* or a *purpose* is largely a matter of personal preference. However, if you think that you know the answer to a research question (i.e., you believe you can predict the answer), you should state a research *hypothesis*:

- It is hypothesized that children of homeless parents are more likely to become homeless adults than are children of housed parents.

Your next step is to take your list of possible questions, purposes, or hypotheses to experts (such as professors who have conducted research) for feedback. Of course, you will want to ask them to help you assess the importance of each in terms of making a contribution to your discipline. In addition, you should ask them to consider the *feasibility* of conducting research on each one. Having conducted research, they are in a better position than you (if you are a first-time researcher) to assess whether one question, purpose, or hypothesis will be inherently more difficult to gather data on than the others. This is important information if you will be conducting research with limited resources. For instance, for the examples in this topic, homeless partici-pants will need to be contacted in person (because they cannot be mailed question-naires). Do you have the resources (and inclination) to personally contact them? If you want to study the "new" homeless, how will you locate them? Will you be able to find a sufficient number of them? Are the homeless likely to be willing to participate in the type of study you are planning? These are examples of *feasibility questions* that would need to be answered before a final selection is made.

Once you have selected research questions, purposes, or hypotheses that are both important and feasible, your next task is to select the appropriate research approach, a topic considered in the next section of this book.

Exercise for Topic 11

1. Write the name of your problem area here.

2. Write the research question(s), purpose(s), or hypothesis(es) on which your research will be based. (Keep in mind that you may wish to have a *set* of closely related ones that will be investigated in a single study. See the example at the end of Topic 7 and the example in the second column of Topic 13.)

3. Get feedback on the importance and feasibility of conducting the research suggested by your research questions, purposes, or hypotheses. Briefly describe your reactions to the feedback. Did it help you to make a final selection?

Part C

Selecting a Research Approach

At this point, you should have selected a problem area and formulated research questions, purposes, or hypotheses on which to base your proposal.

In this part of the book, some important approaches to research (often called *types of research*) will be briefly summarized.[1] Because it is assumed that you have already taken a research methods course (or are taking one currently), the topics in this part of the book are designed to be only reminders of the major approaches and their characteristics. Logically, the selection of an approach should be driven by the nature of the research questions, purposes, or hypotheses. However, the entire process of planning research is interactive. For example, a research purpose might logically lead to a proposal to conduct *qualitative* research; yet, the potential researcher may not have training in how to conduct this type of research—leading to the need to revise or even abandon the initial research purpose in favor of a different one.

---

[1] Methods of research are classified in various ways by different authors of research methods textbooks. Those reviewed in this part are the major ones commonly covered in most textbooks.

Notes

Topic 12

Qualitative Research

The purpose of qualitative research is to gain an *in-depth understanding of purposively selected participants from their perspective*.

The fact that it is *in-depth* rules out the use of typical questionnaires, tests, and psychological scales. Instead, qualitative researchers use techniques such as in-depth semistructured interviews, focus-group discussions, and direct observations over an extended period of time. In fact, sometimes qualitative researchers live with (such as living with a tribe) and work with (such as helping teachers to conduct lessons) their participants. The resulting data do not lend themselves to easy quantification, so qualitative researchers usually report on themes and trends using words instead of statistics.

The use of *purposively selected participants* requires the researcher to have access to particular types of participants who are especially likely to aid in the understanding of a phenomenon. For example, if a research purpose is to understand the motivations of high-achieving African American women in the corporate world, the researcher would need to have access to and deliberately select such women.

Trying to understand participants *from their perspective* requires the researcher to bring an open mind to the research setting. Thus, *hypotheses* are usually an inappropriate basis for qualitative

research. (Remember that a hypothesis is a prediction of a particular outcome, which implies prejudgment.) Rather, qualitative research typically rests on broad research *purposes* (or questions) such as

- The purpose is to explore the intrinsic and extrinsic motivational factors to which high-achieving African American women attribute their success in the corporate world.

Because it is *from the participants' perspective*, after conducting research, qualitative researchers often share their findings with their participants and ask them for feedback (such as having them read and react to the preliminary research report). Such feedback is used in revision of the results sections of their research reports.

Qualitative research is often recommended for new areas of research or areas about which social and behavioral scientists have little previous knowledge. (Note that it is difficult to draw up highly structured instruments such as multiple-choice questionnaires to conduct quantitative research in a new area.) However, qualitative research is also desirable even in well-researched areas whenever in-depth information is needed.

Novice students who have limited knowledge of statistics may be drawn to qualitative research simply because few statistics are required in this type of research. With a little reflection, one can see that this is not a good reason for conducting qualitative research. It is relatively easy to find someone to aid in the quantitative analysis and interpretation of scores obtained through use of objective measures. Getting expert help with sorting through hundreds of pages of transcribed material such as interview verbatims collected in qualitative research is a much more difficult matter. Thus, analyzing the results of qualitative research is usually more difficult than analyzing the data collected in quantitative research.

Exercise for Topic 12

1. Does your research purpose or question lend itself to qualitative research? Explain.

2. At this point, are you planning to propose qualitative research? If yes, will you be able to justify its selection for reasons other than merely a personal distaste for statistics? Explain.

3. If you are planning qualitative research, what type(s) of purposively selected participants do you anticipate using?

Topic 13

Survey Research

The purpose of a typical survey is to *collect information from a sample and generalize it to a larger population.* National political polls are a prime example in which only a sample of potential voters is questioned in order to estimate how all potential voters feel about candidates or issues.

The desire to *generalize* from a survey requires that an adequate sample be drawn. Ideally, a random sample (e.g., drawing names out of a hat) or a stratified random sample (e.g., drawing names out of several hats with particular categories of people, such as men and women, in different hats) should be drawn. In institutional settings, it is often possible for researchers with limited resources to obtain such samples. For instance, with administrative approval, a teacher may be permitted to survey a random sample of students in his or her school in order to generalize to all students in the school.

Researchers interested in noninstitutionalized populations often conduct their surveys by mailing questionnaires. Many of these surveys have notoriously low rates of return (even with follow-up mailings), leaving researchers with information on only those who had sufficient time and interest to respond. If you conduct a survey by mail, you will probably need to warn your readers that the results are highly tentative.

Typically, telephone surveys get a better response rate than mailed ones, and surveys conducted with in-person interviews do even better than telephone surveys.

Here is an example of a set of research hypotheses that lend themselves to survey research:

- It is hypothesized that the following groups of parents will be more in favor of mandatory uniforms in public schools:
  (a) parents with children attending academically troubled schools (as opposed to those with children in high-achieving schools),
  (b) parents with children in schools where there are patterns of student conflict and violence (as opposed to those with children in more peaceful schools), and
  (c) parents whose economic resources are limited (as opposed to wealthier parents).

Notice that these hypotheses require that different groups of parents be compared with each other. For example, the attitudes of wealthier parents toward uniforms will need to be compared with the attitudes of poorer parents. Usually, surveys in which comparisons are made are more interesting than surveys that ask a single global question, such as, "What percentage of parents favor mandatory school uniforms for students in public school?"

Exercise for Topic 13

1. Does your research purpose or question lend itself to survey research? Explain.

2. At this point, are you planning to propose survey research? If yes, will you propose comparing two or more groups?

3. If you are planning survey research, how will you contact the participants (mail, telephone, in person, or electronically such as through the Internet)?

4. If you have a low response rate, are you willing to advise your readers that your results should be viewed with considerable caution? Explain.

Topic 14

Correlational Research

In a simple correlational study, *two quantitative variables are measured* and the degree of relationship between them is determined by *computing a correlation coefficient*.

Most educational and psychological tests and scales yield quantitative scores[1] that could be used in correlational research. The following hypotheses lend themselves to correlational research.

- It is hypothesized that there is a *direct* correlation between College Board SAT scores and freshman GPA.

- It is hypothesized that depression and scholastic achievement are *inversely* related.

A *direct* relationship is one in which those participants with high scores on one variable tend to have high scores on the other variable (and those with low scores on one variable tend to have low scores on the other). For direct relationships, correlation coefficients range from 0.00 (no relationship) to 1.00 (perfect, direct relationship). It follows that values near 1.00 (such as .75 and above) are often called "very strong," and positive values near 0.00 (such as .25 and below) are often called "very weak."

An *inverse* relationship is one in which those participants who score high on one variable (such as being high in depression) score low on the other (such

as being low on scholastic achievement). Values near –1.00 indicate a very strong inverse relationship, while negative values near 0.00 indicate a very weak one.

It is important to note that correlation does not imply causality. For example, even if a strong inverse correlation was found between depression and scholastic achievement, it would not be clear whether high depression caused the low scholastic achievement or something else caused the two to covary together (e.g., a learning disability that might cause low achievement as well as be a cause of depression).

While a simple correlational study is confined to examining two pairs of variables at a time, advanced correlational techniques allow researchers to look at variables in combination. For example, we could use a technique called *multiple regression* to determine how well high school grades predict freshman grades when combined with College Board SAT scores. It would be reasonable to hypothesize that the two predictors *in combination* will be a better predictor than either one individually. Furthermore, regression analysis indicates how important each variable is in making the predictions. For instance, it is a common finding that high school grades are somewhat superior to College Board scores in predicting success in college.

---

[1] They should be quantitative and at the interval or ratio levels of measurement.

Exercise for Topic 14

1. Does your research question, purpose, or hypothesis lend itself to correlational research? Explain.

2. At this point, are you planning to propose correlational research? If yes, will it be "simple" correlational research in which pairs of variables are correlated? (Note that more than one pair might be correlated in a given study.) If yes, name the pair(s) of variables that will be correlated.

3. If you are planning correlational research, will you be correlating some combination of variables (such as high school grades and SAT scores) with one *outcome* variable (such as freshman grades in college)? If yes, name the variables you will combine, and name the outcome variable.

Topic 15

Test Development Research

In this topic, the term *test* is used to stand for any type of instrument, including achievement and aptitude tests, attitude scales, and personality scales.

A basic research proposal might focus on gathering and interpreting data that sheds light on the reliability and validity of a test. A more ambitious research proposal might call for a comparison of the reliabilities and validities of two or more tests, which would assist users in selecting among competing tests.

There are a number of techniques for studying the reliability of a test. An important one is *test-retest reliability*.[1] In this technique, a test is administered to a group of examinees and then administered again to the same examinees, usually with a week or two intervening. Computing a correlation coefficient (see the previous topic) yields what is called a test-retest *reliability coefficient*. Typically, a coefficient of 0.75 or higher is considered adequate.

A concept that is related to reliability is *internal consistency* (sometimes called *internal consistency reliability*). This technique involves correlating all the items in a test with each other and results in a coefficient called *alpha*, whose symbol is α. Like a simple correlation coefficient, α can range from 0.00 to 1.00. A high value of alpha (such as 0.75 or higher) indicates that the items in a test,

on the whole, are measuring the same characteristic, which is usually desirable. However, a high value is not always expected. For instance, for a general achievement test that includes items in a variety of areas such as math, reading, and history, a high value of alpha would not be expected because the content is heterogeneous. For example, one would not expect the math and reading items to correlate highly.

In general terms, *validity* refers to the extent to which a test measures what it is supposed to measure or performs the function that it was designed to serve. Note that validity is relative to the group with which the test is being used and the context in which it is being used. For instance, a test might be valid with one age group but not another.

There are two main approaches to validity.[2] The first is *content validity*, which is determined by having experts examine the items in a test to determine their suitability. For instance, items on a new test of psychomotor development might be examined by developmental psychologists. To the extent that they agree that the items are suitable, the test can be said to have content validity.

The second major approach is an empirical one (i.e., a data-based approach). This involves administering the test and gathering additional data that

---

[1] Other techniques are parallel-forms reliability and split-half reliability.

[2] The traditional approaches are called *content, face, criterion-related,* and *construct validity.*

35

shed light on the validity of the test. An example is administering the College Board's SAT and correlating the scores with grades earned in college. Because the SAT is supposed to predict success in college, such a study would be called a *predictive validity study*. Another example is correlating reading test scores with teachers' judgments of reading ability. To the extent that they are correlated, there is evidence that the test is valid. If the test scores and teachers' judgments are collected at about the same time, the study is a *concurrent validity study*, not a predictive one.

Another example of an empirical approach is to consider theories and common knowledge about a trait and conduct a study to see if the test of the trait operates as expected. For instance, widely accepted theories indicate that anxiety and depression are moderately related. Thus, when validating a new measure of anxiety, one would expect a moderate degree of correlation based on the responses of examinees to the new anxiety measure and an established measure of depression. A very low correlation, on the other hand, would call the validity of the test into question. When theories are used as the basis for empirically validating tests, the studies are known as *construct validity studies*.

Exercise for Topic 15

1. Will test development research be the primary focus of your research? If so, name the test(s) or types of tests involved.

2. If you answered "yes" to Question 1, will you be examining the reliability and validity of an existing test, *or* will you be devising a new test and then gathering reliability and validity data? Explain.

3. If you answered "no" to Question 1, are you considering examining reliability and/or validity within some other type of research project? (For instance, for a study involving job satisfaction and workplace environments, a researcher might examine the internal consistency of the job-satisfaction measure even though that is not the primary focus of the research.)

Topic 16

Experimental Research

In Topic 5, you learned that the purpose of an experiment is to observe the effects of treatments on participants. A set of treatments (such as increasing the number of counselors in some high schools while not increasing them in others) constitutes the *independent variable*. The outcome (such as the number of violent acts per 100 students reported to the principal's office) is the *dependent variable*. Experiments are usually based on hypotheses (as opposed to research questions or purposes) because one would not ordinarily give treatments without expecting some type of response to them. This is a hypothesis that would naturally lead to an experiment:

- It is hypothesized that providing high school students with information sheets on the legal ramifications of substance abuse will result in fewer students reporting that they engage in substance abuse.

When conducting experiments, it is desirable to assign participants at random (such as by drawing names out of a hat) to conditions. For the hypothesis we are considering, ideally about half of the students should be randomly selected to receive the information sheets while the remaining students serve as a control group that does not receive the sheets. Note that the use of randomization to make assignments to treatment creates what is known as a *true experiment*.

When it is not possible to assign at random, useful experiments may still be conducted, provided that great care is used in their execution. For example, perhaps all students in a school will be provided with information sheets on the legal ramifications of substance abuse. In such a situation, a researcher might carefully select another school with a similar student body to serve as a control group. The two schools should be comparable in terms of preexisting rates of substance abuse as well as other important demographics (such as family socioeconomic status, school funding, and so on). To the extent that the researcher can show initial comparability, the results will give a valid indication of the effects of providing an information sheet.

Interesting experiments can be conducted by examining two or more independent variables at the same time. For example, we might establish four groups of students as follows:

	Information sheet provided	No information sheet provided
Classroom discussion of substance abuse	Group A	Group B
No classroom discussion of substance abuse	Group C	Group D

This would allow a researcher to examine two issues simultaneously. For this example, for instance, a researcher might hypothesize that Group A, which receives both the information sheet and the classroom discussion, will report less substance abuse than any of the other groups. Furthermore, the researcher might hypothesize that Group D, which receives no information sheet and no classroom discussion, will report more substance abuse than any of the other groups.

Exercise for Topic 16

1. Does your research hypothesis suggest an experiment? If yes, state your hypothesis. (Note: You may have two or more closely related hypotheses for a given study.)

2. If you will be conducting an experiment, do you anticipate assigning the participants at random to treatment conditions (i.e., conducting a true experiment)?

3. If you will be conducting an experiment and do *not* anticipate assigning the participants at random to treatment conditions, will you compare the experimental group with a *comparable* control group? If yes, on what types of variables do you plan to seek comparability?

Topic 17
Causal-Comparative Research

In the previous topic, you learned how cause-and-effect relationships might be examined by conducting an experiment. Sometimes, we are interested in identifying a cause *after* the effect or outcome has already been observed. For instance, we might observe that a large number of students dropped out of a local high school last year. Note that dropping out is an outcome or *dependent variable*. Research might be conducted to try to establish the cause (the *independent variable*). This would require *causal-comparative* research in which we look for the cause of some observation by looking to the past and comparing groups.

For example, we might have the following research purpose:

- The purpose is to explore the reasons for dropping out by interviewing dropouts with attention to school-related variables such as the availability of counseling, perceptions of teachers' helpfulness, and other support services. As a point of comparison, nondropouts who are comparable on major sociodemographic variables will also be interviewed, and their responses will be compared with those who dropped out.

A major danger in causal-comparative research is that an apparent cause may be coincidental to the true cause or may even be the result of the true cause. This is illustrated by this simplified example:

Example

Many employees who attended a large company picnic became ill with severe gastrointestinal distress. As a point of comparison, researchers contacted those who attended the picnic (a comparable group) but who did not get ill. They found that those who became ill ate a green salad while those who did not become ill did not eat the salad. At this point, the salad seemed to be the culprit (cause). However, if they had stopped at this point, they would not have found the true cause. As it turned out, raw chicken was first cut up for the picnic on the same unwashed cutting boards that the salad ingredients were later cut up on. Salmonella associated with the chicken—and not the salad—was the cause.

As a general rule, causal-comparative research should be undertaken only if an experiment cannot be conducted because researchers have more control over the participants' environment when conducting an experiment than when conducting a causal-comparative study. This extra measure of control allows those conducting experiments to rule out many alternative explanations for their results. However, for ethical and legal reasons, there are many types of treatments that cannot be given and must be studied after the fact. Here are a few examples of causal research questions that are not amenable to experimentation because we would not want to deliberately subject participants to the treatments implied by them:

- Do children who view violent media at a very early age tend to be more violent as teenagers than those who do not view it?

- Does incarceration of first-time offenders with dangerous prisoners, guilty of serious offenses, increase the odds that the first-time offenders will become hardened criminals?

In neither of these cases would we want to deliberately subject participants to the implied treatments (such as showing violent media to very young children). Instead, we will need to work backwards with the causal-comparative method. For example, we might identify a group of violent teenagers and a group of nonviolent teenagers who are comparable in terms of demographics such as income, ethnicity, and so on. Comparing the amount of media violence each group was exposed to when they were young would give us some tentative answers to the research question.

Exercise for Topic 17

1. Does your research hypothesis suggest a causal-comparative study? Explain.

2. If you answered "yes" to Question 1, what is your reason for conducting a causal-comparative study instead of an experiment?

3. If you answered "yes" to Question 1, do you anticipate any difficulties in interpreting the results that you would not have if you conduct an experiment? Explain.

Topic 18

Program Evaluation

Students who have access to program directors might consider proposing program evaluation as their research project. The local efforts of large, national programs such as Big Brothers and Head Start can be evaluated as well as small local programs. For instance, many colleges have programs to help reduce students' consumption of alcohol, to help students with their access to the Internet, to help freshmen get off to a good start, and so on. Evaluation of such programs can provide useful feedback to program directors.

One major aspect of program evaluation that makes it unique among research approaches is that a comprehensive evaluation often begins with a *needs assessment*, which is a study of what individuals perceive their needs to be as well as what type of program(s) they think will help meet their needs. A needs assessment is conducted during the programs' planning stages, and the data generated by the needs assessment are used in a proposal to get funding for a new program. The data can consist of responses to a survey or be obtained through qualitative methods such as semistructured interviews.

The second major aspect of program evaluation is *formative evaluation* (also called *process evaluation*). There are two prongs to formative evaluation. First, formative evaluation is used to examine *implementation* of the program.

For instance, for a mentoring program for college freshmen, an evaluator might gather implementation data on questions such as, "Were the mentors properly trained?" "How effective was the training?" "Were all freshmen assigned a mentor?" and so on. Sometimes implementation data are collected using qualitative methods, but more often quantitative methods are used.

The second prong of formative evaluation focuses on *progress*. For this, data are collected on the extent to which the clients being served by the program are progressing in the desired direction. For instance, for a mentoring program, an evaluator might gather data to answer questions such as, "What are the freshmen's initial reactions to their mentors?" and "At the end of the first month of the semester, do freshmen report being more well adjusted due to the mentorship?" Sometimes data on program recipients' progress are collected using qualitative methods, but more often quantitative methods are used.

The overall purpose of formative evaluation, then, is to gather data that help the program to get off to a good start (as envisioned by the program developers) and to stay on track.

The third major aspect of program evaluation is *summative evaluation*. Typically, this concerns the overall effectiveness of the program near its end or near the end of each year's implementation. For the example in this topic, an evaluator might conduct a summative evaluation by gathering data near the end of the school year on the extent to which freshmen report being helped by the mentors, how the mentors were especially effective (or ineffective), and the students' recommendations for future mentoring programs.

When conducting summative evaluations, it is usually quite useful to have a control or comparison group, such as a group of freshmen who do not have mentors. However, this is not always possible in practice. For instance, it may be the college's policy to supply mentors to all freshmen, leaving none to serve as a control group.

Quantitative data are usually gathered in summative evaluations, although qualitative data can also be useful.

When proposing program evaluation research, it is not always necessary to propose research on all aspects. For instance, a proposal might be written to collect only needs-assessment data.

Exercise for Topic 18

1. Are you considering writing a proposal to conduct a program evaluation? If so, name the program and explain your interest in it.

2. If you answered "yes" to Question 1, do you plan to conduct (1) a needs assessment, (2) a formative evaluation, *and* (3) a summative evaluation? If not, which one or two of the three aspects of evaluation will you propose?

3. If you answered "yes" to Question 1, do you plan to gather quantitative data? Qualitative data? A combination of quantitative and qualitative data? Explain.

Part D

Organizing and Evaluating Literature

At this point, you should have selected a problem area and formulated research questions, purposes, or hypotheses on which to base your proposal. In addition, you should have selected a research approach. Finally, you should have conducted an extensive search of the literature with an emphasis on locating research articles published in academic journals. (See Appendix A for information on searching for literature electronically.)

A typical research proposal begins with an introduction that relies heavily on the research literature on your topic. Before beginning to write, you should review, evaluate, and organize the literature you have collected. These tasks are covered in this part of the book.

Notes

Topic 19
Organizing Literature by Topics

Begin by sorting the research articles you have collected according to the topic(s) they cover.[1] Because many research articles may cover more than one topic you wish to review, this task is a bit more difficult than you might anticipate. Here is a way to simplify the task:

A. Give each article a number. It does not matter what number you give each one as long as each article has a different number.

B. As you read the articles, begin preparing a tentative list of subtopics that you might cover in your literature review. Revise this as you proceed through the literature. Get feedback on this list.

C. Obtain a set of 3-by-5 note cards, and write the name of a single subtopic on each one. On the card, write the article number(s) that contain information on the topic. Note that one article may cover more than one topic.

Consider this simple example: Suppose your research hypothesis is that learning through apprenticeships in workplaces results in more learning than self-directed learning does. Following are some of the *topics* that might be written on the cards.[2]

Topics for a Set of Cards
1. Conceptualizations of workplace learning
2. Definitions of workplace learning
3. Self-directed learning
4. Learning through apprenticeships
5. Characteristics of workplaces as learning environments
6. Workplace support of learning
7. Theories relating to workplace learning

Suppose that the article you labeled as No. 1 contains an especially good definition of workplace learning and also reports on the use of apprenticeships. You should write "No. 1" on the card for definitions (for Topic 2 in the list above) *and* also write No. 1 on the card for apprenticeships (Topic 4 in the list above). Thus, article No. 1 becomes associated with two different topic cards.

If you are dealing with an especially large body of literature, you may wish to develop subcategories under the major topics. For example, Topic 7 might have two cards: one for cognitive theories and one for social theories.

Depending on the nature of the literature you are reviewing, you might want to have a separate card for each approach to research (see Part C of this book). For example, you might have a card for qualitative research, one for survey research, and so on. You might also wish to have a card for various types of participants in the research. For instance,

---

[1] See Appendix A for information on locating literature electronically.
[2] The topics for this example are based on material in Smith, P. J. (2003). Workplace learning and flexible delivery. *Review of Educational Research, 73*, 53–88.

there might be one card for *high school* (studies of cooperative learning with high school students) and *college* (studies with college students). Note that those with college students are more relevant to the hypothesis we are considering but that the literature on high school students might contain important information you wish to review.

The system suggested here will prepare you to organize your literature review *by topics*. In other words, it will help you to write a literature review that moves from topic to topic with appropriate citations to the literature. Note that a given article may be cited at one or more points in a literature review.

Exercise for Topic 19

1. List some major topics that relate to each of your research questions, purposes, or hypotheses. (These should be based on your initial reading of the literature.)

2. As you read the literature again, consider whether you should add more topics or subtopics. If so, list them here.

3. Number the articles you have collected, and prepare a set of topic cards as described earlier. Write your reactions to the process here. Did you find some things hard to classify? Did you get a better understanding of your literature as a result of following the recommendations in this topic? Explain.

Topic 20

Evaluating Research Literature

In preparation for writing the introduction and literature review for your proposal, you should evaluate the empirical studies located through your literature search. Evaluations are important because, other things being equal, you will want to emphasize the stronger studies while warning your readers about extremely weak studies that you cite.[1]

Because it is assumed that you have taken a research methods course in which you learned how to distinguish strong studies from weak ones, the following material is designed to be only a refresher on three of the most salient issues in evaluating research.

First is the issue of *sampling*. *Quantitative researchers* emphasize the use of solid sampling techniques such as simple random or stratified random sampling so that the results of the study can be generalized with confidence to the population from which the sample was drawn. However, many researchers lack the resources or cooperation from participants to obtain such samples, so you will need to decide which studies have better samples. Often, this will be clear, such as when one researcher has a high rate of response to a mailed survey while another one has a low rate.

When evaluating samples, also consider the diversity of the samples (even if they are biased). For example, a study on communication pattern differences between husbands and wives that is based only on married college students has a less diverse sample than one with a sample consisting of college students *and* married individuals who reside in the larger community (often called a *community sample*).

Also, consider how closely the samples used in the literature correspond to the samples you will be using. For example, if you will be studying college students enrolled in a college-level mathematics class, research based on middle-school students in mathematics might not apply directly to your study.

When evaluating the samples used by *qualitative researchers*, ask yourself if the samples are truly purposive (see Topic 12) *or* merely convenience samples consisting of people who happened to be convenient to the researchers. Obviously, a purposive sample is superior to a convenience sample.

The second issue is *measurement*. Do the researchers provide you with information on the reliability and validity of their measurement techniques (see Topic 15)? Keep in mind that no measure should be presumed perfect. Do the measures seem suitable for the research purposes? Have the researchers used multiple methods/sources to measure crucial variables? For example, a study on designated driving that relies solely on self-reports by participants is less strong than

---

[1] Methods for critiquing weak studies are discussed in Topic 26.

one that supplements self-reports with direct observations of behavior. Multiple sources of information can also be obtained by asking a variety of sources to report on the same phenomenon. For example, a study in which students self-report on their academic motivation will be stronger if teachers and parents are also asked to report on the same students' motivation.

The third issue is *conclusions*. Check to determine the extent to which the conclusions reached by the researchers are substantiated by the research. You will not want to cite strongly stated conclusions based on weak studies without warning your readers of the weaknesses.

Exercise for Topic 20

1. Select one of the research articles that you identified in your literature search.

   A. Briefly evaluate the sample:

   B. Briefly evaluate the measurement procedures:

   C. Briefly evaluate the conclusions in light of the research methodology:

2. Select another one of the research articles that you identified in your literature search.

   A. Briefly evaluate the sample:

   B. Briefly evaluate the measurement procedures:

   C. Briefly evaluate the conclusions in light of the research methodology:

Topic 21
Considering the History of a Topic

In your literature review, you may want to provide a historical perspective to help establish the context in which you will be conducting research. This is especially true if you are writing a proposal for a thesis or dissertation because your committee may want to be sure that you know *where you are coming from* as well as *where you hope to go*.

To gain a historical perspective, put the research articles you have collected in chronological order from oldest to newest. Then, examine them to look for changes over time. Be especially careful to notice changes of the following types:

- *Changes in definitions*. For example, have definitions of physical child abuse changed to include milder forms of abuse (such as spanking) over time? If so, this may account for the increased reporting of child abuse cases over time. You will need to decide whether to use the newer or older definition(s) and inform your readers of the basis for your decision. Note that it is often desirable to use an existing definition rather than trying to develop a new one because existing definitions are often written by experts on the topic in question.

- *New terminology*. For example, there is a long history of studies of *burnout* and stress among psychotherapists. However, a newer term such as *vicarious traumatization* (psychotherapists themselves becoming trauma-tized through their empathy with traumatized clients) may signal a new line of thought and research on this topic. You may wish to point out how research on burnout differs from research based on the newer term.

- *Changes in theoretical underpinnings*. For example, do the authors of older research trace its origins to Freud while newer research emphasizes Ellis's theory? If so, you will want to point this out to your readers.

In addition, you should look for *key players*—those who have built a career conducting research on your topic. They are usually easy to spot because it is likely that they have authored or co-authored a number of articles on the topic, and they will be frequently cited in the literature. If you find that there is one essential key player, you may want to briefly trace how this person has contributed to and progressed the research in your problem area when you write your literature review.

In your quest for a historical overview on your topic, you may find assistance in the writings of others. Other researchers sometimes provide historical overviews in the introductions to their research articles. You might use these as the starting point for writing your own historical overview.

Exercise for Topic 21

1. Put the research articles you have collected into chronological order and examine them. Have the definitions of key terms in your area changed over time? Explain.

2. Has new terminology been introduced? Explain.

3. Have there been changes in the theoretical underpinnings of the area you will be studying? Explain.

4. Is there a key player? Do you think it will be worthwhile to trace his or her historical contributions to your area of research? Explain.

Part E

Writing the Introduction and Literature Review

Having studied Parts A through D of this book, you are now ready to begin writing. Before beginning, however, determine whether the introduction needs to be separate from the literature review or whether the literature review should be integrated with the introductory remarks. The sample proposals near the end of this book illustrate the latter.

Topic 22 in this part of the book provides suggestions for those who will be writing a separate introduction, which is often required of thesis and dissertation students. Topic 23 deals with the integration of an introduction with a literature review. The remaining topics deal with the development of an effective literature review.

The following outline shows the components of a typical research proposal. We will refer to this outline at the beginning of each of the remaining parts of this book to help you get the big picture of where you are and where you will be going while writing your proposal.

I.	Introduction	←*You are here.*
II.	Literature Review*	←*You are here.*
III.	Method	
	A. Participants	
	B. Instrumentation	
	C. Procedures	
IV.	Analysis	
V.	Discussion**	

*May be integrated with the Introduction.
**Followed by writing a title and an abstract as well as developing
  a timeline.

Notes

Topic 22

A Separate Introduction

In research reports in academic journals, the literature review is usually integrated with the introductory statements. In theses and dissertations, it is more common to present an introduction in the first chapter and the literature review in the second chapter.

Following are some guidelines for writing a separate introduction, which might be required in a thesis, dissertation, or term project. Note that some of the guidelines will be explored again in more detail in later topics.

- The first paragraph should usually introduce the *specific* problem area in which you will be conducting research. For instance, if your problem area is the effects of rewards on creative behavior in the classroom, do *not* start with a discussion of the importance of education in a technological society. Instead, start by discussing why educators are interested in fostering creativity and ways in which they use rewards.

- As soon as possible, establish that your problem area is important. This can be done in a number of ways. For example, you might be able to point out that government agencies or prominent scholars have called for additional research in your area. You might also have some statistics showing that many people are affected by the problem you are proposing to investigate.

- Provide definitions of key terms early in the introduction. For example, how is *creativity* defined by other scholars? What definition will be used in your research?

- Provide an overview of the important points and trends in the literature you have read. Do not get too specific because the literature review will be presented in the second chapter. However, it would be appropriate to make statements such as, "As the literature review that follows shows, several experiments suggest that creativity is not enhanced by the provision of material rewards. This finding is consistent with the theory of...." (In the separate literature review, you will want to cite the specific experiments and provide some details on them.)

- Provide an overview of your proposed research methodology. What *type* of research are you proposing (e.g., qualitative, survey, and so on)? Why did you select that type?

- Point out why your particular study is needed. For instance, given that a number of studies on the effects of rewards on creativity have already been conducted, how will your study advance knowledge in this area? Will you use a better sample? Will you examine a different type of creativity? Will you measure creativity with a new instrument? These issues usually should be addressed in general terms in the introduction because the specifics will be addressed later, in the proposal for the section on the proposed research methods.

- Discuss the broad implications of your proposed research in general terms. Note that a detailed discussion should be provided in the last section of your proposal (i.e., the discussion section, covered later in this book).

By incorporating these suggestions, your introduction will provide a broad overview of your proposal, which will show your readers the big picture before they begin reading for details in the proposal's subsequent sections.

Exercise for Topic 22

1. Determine whether you are required to write an introduction that is separate from the literature review. If you are, what guidelines, if any, exist for this activity?

2. Prepare a topic outline of what you will cover in your introduction. Refer to any guidelines that you have been given as well as to the suggestions in this topic.

3. Get feedback from instructors and colleagues on the topic outline you have written. Revise it in light of their suggestions.

4. Write a first draft of the introduction and have it reviewed.

An Integrated Introduction and Literature Review

The previous topic provided guidelines for writing a separate introduction. If you will be writing an introduction integrated with the literature review, you will be covering the same material discussed in Topic 22. However, you will be relying heavily on the literature for specifics to support your points.

As in the case of a separate introduction, the first paragraph should introduce the *specific* problem area—not some broad general topic. Also, use the first paragraph or two to establish the importance of your research problem, using specifics from the literature to support your contention. The first paragraph of a proposal is important because a strong beginning is likely to convince readers that the remainder of the proposal is worthy of careful consideration. It is so important that the next topic in this book is devoted to writing the first paragraph.

In an integrated introduction and literature review, key terms should be defined early. Usually, conceptual (dictionary-like) definitions are sufficient. Operational definitions that describe how you identified or measured the variables will be presented later in the proposal. The following example presents a conceptual definition that was drawn from another research article. Note that it is not necessary to create new definitions if previously published ones are adequate.[1]

Example

> Empowerment is defined as making someone stronger and more confident, especially in controlling their life and claiming their rights (Pearsall & Hanks, 1998).[2]

Following the definitions, literature should be cited that shows the development of intellectual thought in your subject and a discussion of the major findings in previous research. The remaining topics in this part of the book provide guidance on how to do this. At this point, however, note that an effective literature review presents the literature *from your point of view*. In other words, you are responsible for organizing the literature into various topical groups and for showing your reader how it fits together (or fails to do so). In order to do this, you will need to add your own commentary and not simply write a string of summaries of individual studies.

As you write the literature review, point out which studies are most closely allied with your proposed study. In addi-

---

[1] All academic fields have dictionaries that provide definitions of terms written by experts in those fields. Consult your reference librarian for information on dictionaries such as *The Social Work Dictionary*, published by the National Association of Social Workers.

[2] Mok, E., Martinson, I., & Wong, T. K. S. (2004). Individual empowerment among Chinese cancer patients in Hong Kong. *Western Journal of Nursing Research, 26*, 59–75.

tion, discuss how your study is similar to (as well as different from) those previously published.

Typically, a literature review (whether it is written as a separate section or is integrated with the introduction) ends with the specific research questions, purposes, or hypotheses that form the basis of your proposal. If your literature review is well constructed, your questions, purposes, or hypotheses will be seen by your readers as a natural outgrowth of the literature you have reviewed for them.

If you have not done so already, examine the beginnings of the model research proposals near the end of this book for examples of introductions integrated with literature reviews.

Exercise for Topic 23

1. What key terms will you be defining at the conceptual level? Will you be creating new definitions or using those suggested by others? Explain.

2. Do you have a *point of view* on the literature you have read (i.e., do you have a sense of what it means *as a whole*)? Explain.

3. Do you anticipate that you will be able to show your readers how your research questions, purposes, or hypotheses naturally flow from the literature you are reviewing? Explain.

Topic 24

Writing the First Paragraph(s)

The first paragraph of your proposal (whether it is a separate introduction or an integrated introduction and literature review) should identify the specific problem area. In Example 1, the "poor beginning" of the beginning of the first paragraph is not as specific as the "improved version" for a study on the validity of the Graduate Record Examination.

Example 1

Poor beginning (not sufficiently specific):
The issue of college admissions has become of increasing concern to students, parents, and the public. This is especially true in the new millennium, in which many more students will be enrolling in college and eventually going on to graduate school.

Improved version (specific to the research topic):
The Graduate Record Examinations (GRE) General Test is a standardized test of verbal, quantitative, and analytical reasoning that is designed, primarily, to facilitate admissions to U.S. graduate schools. Since its inception in 1949, the original measure and several revisions have been widely used and frequently studied (e.g., see Briel, O'Neill, & Scheuneman, 1993...).[1]

The first paragraphs normally should establish (or start to establish) the importance of the problem.

One technique for establishing the current need for a study in an area is to cite specific statistics indicating the numbers of people affected by the problem that will be investigated in the research. This was done by the authors of the following example.

Example 2
It is estimated that 14% of total mortality (300,000 deaths annually) could be prevented through lifestyle improvements such as regular physical activity (McGinnis & Foege, 1993). Regular physical activity has been shown to help prevent and control a variety of chronic diseases and conditions, including cardiovascular disease (CVD), hypertension....[2]

Note that the statement in Example 2 is much stronger than a statement without specific statistics such as, "Many deaths could be prevented through lifestyle improvements such as regular physical activity."

Like Example 2, the following example shows a first paragraph that is both specific to the research problem and supported by specific statistics.

Example 3
Alcohol consumption among students is one of the primary health concerns for U.S. colleges and universities. Heavy consumption of alcohol is common among undergraduate students, with an estimated 48.6% of men and 40.9% of women classified as binge drinkers, according to the 2001 Harvard College Alcohol Study....[3]

---

[1] Powers, D. E. (2004). Validity of Graduate Record Examinations (GRE) General Test scores for admissions to colleges of veterinary medicine. *Journal of Applied Psychology, 89,* 208–219.

[2] Collins, R., Lee, R. E., Albright, C. L., & King, A. C. (2004). Ready to be physically active? The effects of a course preparing low-income multiethnic women to be more physically active. *Health Education & Behavior, 31,* 47–64.

[3] Usdan, S. L., Schumacher, J. E., & Bernhardt, J. M. (2004). Impaired driving behaviors among college students: A comparison of Web-based daily assessment and retrospective timeline followback. *Journal of Alcohol and Drug Education, 48,* 34–50.

Be prepared to write and rewrite the first paragraph(s) until you have a strong, specific beginning. Get feedback from others, and carefully consider their assessments during this process.

Exercise for Topic 24

1. Will you be using one of the techniques discussed in this topic in the first paragraph of your proposal? Explain.

2. From whom will you get feedback on your first paragraph?

Topic 25

Using a Topic Outline

Developing and following a topic outline while writing helps to produce focused, logical prose. When dealing with a large amount of literature, it will also help you to avoid becoming overwhelmed by the volume of material to be covered.

In Topic 19, you were instructed to organize the literature you collected by topic, to put the name of each topic on a card, and to write the article numbers that touched on each topic on the cards. At this point, try sorting and resorting the cards to establish the order in which the topics will be addressed in your literature review. Then prepare a topic outline.

Here is a sample topic outline for a literature review:[1]

Problem area: Parents' feelings about the amount of time spent with their children

1. Name specific problem area
2. Amount of time parents spend with their children: historical and contemporary statistics
3. Factors associated with feelings about time with children
   A. Gender of parents
      (1) Mothers' feelings
      (2) Fathers' feelings
   B. Age of children
      (1) Preschoolers
      (2) School-aged children
      (3) Adolescents
   C. Parental employment
   D. Family structure
      (1) Single-parent households
      (2) Two-parent households
   E. Other factors

(1) Race/ethnicity
(2) Parents' ages
(3) Socioeconomic status
(4) Gender differences in valuing science (interest)
4. Statement of the research questions

Next, you should begin writing while referring to your topic cards for appropriate references. Note that more than one reference may be used to substantiate a given point. In the following example, for instance, two studies are cited to support the statement in the second sentence.

Example

Studies suggest that there are some cultural variations in parenting and children's time use by race and ethnicity. Black families tend to emphasize the importance of involvement in church activities and achievement at school (Julian, McKenry, & McKelvey, 1994; Rashid, 1985), and, indeed, black children spend more time than white children at church and school (Hofferth & Sandberg, 2001). Hispanic families tend to value children highly and integrate them into their daily lives (Slonim, 1991); hence, compared with white children, Hispanic children spend more time on housework....[2]

If you are writing a long review (say, three or more pages), it is very desirable to use major headings and subheadings within the review to help your readers understand its structure. The topics in your topic outline can be used as such headings. Note that writing short essays about one subtopic at a time makes the overall task of writing a long review easier.

---

[1] This topic outline is loosely based on the work of Milkie, M. A., Mattingly, M. J., Nomaguchi, K. M., Bianchi, S. M., & Robinson, J. P. (2004). The time squeeze: Parental statuses and feelings about time with children. *Journal of Marriage and the Family, 66,* 739–761.

---

[2] Ibid., p. 742.

For a long literature review, consider writing a summary of the literature review. Usually, such a summary should be placed just before the statement of research purposes, questions, or hypotheses that conclude the review.

Exercise for Topic 25

1. Write a topic outline on which to base your literature review.

2. Do you anticipate using major headings/subheadings within your review? Explain.

3. Will you end your review with a statement of your specific research questions, purposes, or hypotheses? If not, where will it be placed?

Topic 26

Being Selective and Critical

The literature covered in a typical research proposal should be selective. Generally, you should select those articles that bear most directly on your research plans. If there are many of this type, select and emphasize those that have the strongest research methodology (see Topic 20 for reminders on evaluating research literature). Other things being equal, more recent research should be emphasized over older research except when you are providing a historical overview of your research topic (see Topic 21).

If you will be citing only some of the studies that support a statement, use "e.g.," meaning "for example," as is done in Example 1.

Example 1

Factors that have been found to predict individual differences in job performance include cognitive ability (e.g., Hunter & Hunter, 1984), conscientiousness (e.g., Barrick & Mount, 1991), goal orientation (e.g., Button, Mathieu, & Zajac, 1996), and motivation (e.g., Ambrose & Kulik, 1999).[1]

Note that if you are writing a research proposal for a thesis or dissertation, your committee may expect you to be comprehensive in your citations to demonstrate that you are familiar with all the literature that has a direct bearing on your proposal. Thus, you may not be permitted to use the technique of citing only examples of studies that support a certain point.

In addition to being selective, you should also be critical. You can warn your readers of tenuous results with various techniques, such as referring to a weak study as a pilot study or by referring to certain specific weaknesses, such as having a very small sample. Example 2 illustrates these techniques.

Example 2

In a series of pilot studies, X was found to precede Y in most cases (Smith, 2004).

Based on interviews with just five teenage boys, Jones (2003) found that A is stronger than B.

You should also consider critiquing groups of studies on a given topic if they all have a common weakness (or strength). Example 3 illustrates this.

Example 3

Almost all the available data on this topic were collected using mailed surveys with low response rates. Hence, little is known about the views of nonrespondents.

You should also point out gaps in the literature. Are there unstudied groups and variables? Have researchers tackled your problem only from one theoretical perspective and not others? A strong feature of any proposal is being able to show that the proposed study will help to fill a gap in our knowledge of an important topic.

---

[1] Yeo, G. B., & Neal, A. (2004). A multilevel analysis of effort, practice, and performance: Effects of ability, conscientiousness, and goal orientation. *Journal of Applied Psychology, 89,* 231–247.

Exercise for Topic 26

1. How selective will you be when you write your literature review? Will you cite all the studies? Only the most important ones? Explain.

2. Do you have sufficient command of the literature that you have collected to be critical? Are there groups of articles with a common weakness? Explain.

3. Are there gaps in the literature? Will your study fill the gaps? Explain.

Part F

Proposing a Sample

In a typical research proposal, the introduction and literature review are followed by a description of the proposed research methodology. This section of the report is usually identified with the major heading "Method," followed by a subheading "Participants" or "Subjects." It is in this section that you should describe your proposed sample. Note that "Participants" should be used if the individuals in your study are freely participating with knowledge of the purposes of the research. On the other hand, "Subjects" is more appropriate if the individuals do not know they are being studied or are coerced to be in a study.[1] Some researchers prefer to use the subheading "Respondents" when referring to individuals who have responded to a survey.

> I.   Introduction
> II. Literature Review*
> III. Method
>   A. Participants   ←*You are here.*
>   B. Instrumentation
>   C. Procedures
> IV. Analysis
> V.   Discussion**

*May be integrated with the Introduction.
**Followed by writing a title and an abstract as well as developing a timeline.

---

[1] For ethical and legal reasons, most researchers avoid coercion to obtain a sample. However, there are many examples of subjects being observed in public places without knowledge that they are part of a study. For example, we might observe drivers' behavior in parking lots or teenagers' behavior in shopping malls.

Notes

Topic 27
Sampling in Qualitative Research

In Topic 12, you learned that the purpose of qualitative research is to gain an *in-depth understanding of purposively selected participants from their perspective.* Hence, if you will be conducting qualitative research, you should propose to purposively select participants who meet *criteria* that will yield a sample likely to provide the types of information you need to achieve your research purpose.

Consider an example: Suppose your research purpose is to explore the nature and extent of the psychological and social support new teachers receive from other teachers, school administrators, and other school personnel with attention to the relationship between such support and their satisfaction in their jobs. Obviously, one *criterion* you will use is that the teacher-participants will need to be new teachers. Other criteria you might consider are (1) Will you restrict the sample to fully trained and credentialed (i.e., licensed) teachers, or will you include teachers who are teaching on an emergency credential (not fully trained and licensed)? (2) Will you include teachers who teach in urban, suburban, and rural areas, or will you restrict the sample to those in just one type of area? (3) Will you include both male and female teachers? (4) Will you include elementary, middle school, and high school teachers or restrict the sample to just one category? After thinking through such questions, you should prepare a

statement of the criteria for selection of participants to include in your proposal. Following is an example of such a statement.

Example
Criteria for participant selection will be as follows. The teacher-participants must be fully credentialed and in their first or second year of teaching at the elementary level in a large urban school district. They will be selected without regard to gender. However, it is anticipated that there will be more females than males in the sample because the teaching profession at the elementary level is female-dominated.

Next, you should propose a method for locating participants who meet your selection criteria. Will you telephone elementary school principals throughout an urban school district and request their cooperation in identifying teachers who meet your criteria? Will you use just the three teachers who meet these criteria at your neighborhood elementary school, where you are already on friendly terms with the principal? Either of these possibilities is acceptable, but note that the second one will limit your study to teachers in one particular school. Will those who will be evaluating your proposal find this acceptable? Is there something special about this school (e.g., a school with a reputation for high academic achievement) that makes it especially interesting? If so, you should address this issue in your proposal.

Note that sample size is usually not a major issue in qualitative research. Because you will be striving for in-depth information, you will probably not be expected to use a large number of participants. It is more important to spend enough time with a small number than to work superficially with a large number of participants.

Note that qualitative researchers sometimes start with a small number of participants and continue adding more until they reach the point of redundancy (i.e., when they find that the newly added participants are not contributing information or insights beyond those already obtained from previous participants). However, in your proposal, you should consider stating an anticipated number of participants or a ballpark number that would be the maximum you believe you could work with during your timeframe and with your resources. This is especially true of thesis and dissertation students who will want feedback from their committees regarding their proposed sample size.

Exercise for Topic 27

1. If you are proposing qualitative research, write your research purpose or question here:

2. Write a statement that names the criteria you propose to use in selecting participants.

3. Write a statement that describes how you propose to locate participants who meet your criteria.

4. Do you have an anticipated sample size? Explain. Do you have a maximum number in mind with which you have the resources to work? Explain. Will you sample to the point of redundancy? Explain.

Topic 28

Random Sampling

In quantitative research, the ideal is to identify a population of interest and sample from it at random. Random sampling gives each person in the population an equal and independent chance of being selected. A sample drawn at random is, by definition, unbiased. Drawing names out of a hat is the basic way to obtain a random sample. Equivalent results can be obtained using a table of random numbers or computer-generated random samples. Be careful to distinguish between *random sampling* and *accidental sampling* (also known as convenience sampling). Selecting individuals who happen to be available is *not* random sampling.

In order to give every individual an equal chance, you will need to know the identities of each one of them as well as how to contact them (e.g., an address). Often, researchers have this knowledge for only a subset of the population of interest. This is called the *sampling frame*, that is, the set of individuals accessible to a researcher. For example, suppose your research purpose calls for contacting all students who have graduated from a school during the past 10 years. You will probably find that the alumni records (with current addresses) are incomplete because the alumni office has lost contact with many of the graduates. Thus, your sample will need to be drawn from the subset for which current addresses are available. The following example shows how this might be proposed.

Example
The population for this study consists solely of graduates of Eisenhower High School from 1992 through 2003. However, the alumni office estimates that it has current addresses for only 71% ($n = 6,745$) of this population. These 6,745 graduates will constitute the sampling frame from which a simple random sample of 11% ($n = 742$) will be contacted by mail to participate in the study.

Notice the use of the term *simple random sample* in the example. The adjective *simple* refers to drawing the sample in one step from the entire sampling frame. In contrast, in a *stratified random sample*, the individuals in the sampling frame are divided into known subgroups and a fixed percentage is drawn from each subgroup. For instance, if we divide those in the sampling frame into males and females and draw 11% of the males and 11% of the females, we have stratified on the basis of gender, which results in a sample that is representative in terms of this characteristic. If you will be using stratified random sampling, you should indicate the basis for stratification (e.g., gender) in your proposal. The last sentence of the example above could be rewritten as follows: "These 6,745 graduates will constitute the sampling frame from which a sample of 11% ($n = 742$) stratified on the basis of gender will be drawn."

Other methods of sampling as well as the issue of sample size are covered in subsequent topics in this part of the book.

Exercise for Topic 28

1. Do you know the identities and have contact information for the entire population of interest to you? If not, do you have this information on a sampling frame within the population? Explain.

2. Do you plan to draw a simple random sample for your study? If so, write a first draft of a statement to that effect.

3. Do you plan to draw a stratified random sample for your study? If so, write a first draft of a statement to that effect.

Other Methods of Sampling: I

Although random sampling is preferred in quantitative research (see Topic 28), quantitative researchers often do not have sufficient knowledge of a population or do not have the resources to obtain such a sample. In this topic, we will consider two other methods of sampling and how they might be proposed.

Suppose your research purpose is to explore the nutritional needs of injecting drug abusers who have not had contact with law enforcement and have not sought treatment for their addiction. Obviously, there is no master list of such individuals (with contact information) from which you could draw a random sample. However, if you could identify even a few such individuals (perhaps through people who are currently seeking treatment), these few might put you in touch with others who could then provide you with additional names so that your sample grows geometrically, like a snowball. In fact, this type of sampling is known as *snowball sampling*. Example 1 shows how this might be proposed.

Example 1

To obtain a sample of injecting drug abusers who have not had contact with law enforcement and have not sought treatment, clients at a public and a private drug abuse treatment center will be asked to contact personal acquaintances who meet the criteria for participation in this study. Specifically, the directors of the two treatment centers have agreed to allow their social workers to distribute flyers to their clients. The flyers will briefly describe the purposes of the proposed research and will include information on how the researchers can be contacted by phone. The flyers will guarantee anonymity and will offer a token reward of $20 for participation in a half-hour interview. Those who respond to this offer will be asked to nominate additional potential participants. This snowball technique will be used until a sample of at least 24 participants is obtained.

For practical reasons, researchers sometimes plan to use samples that happen to be readily available to them. These are known as *convenience* or *accidental* samples. If you will be using such a sample, any generalizations from it to a population will have to be made with great caution. Usually, it is best to address this issue directly when describing your proposed sample, as illustrated in Example 2.

Example 2

The participants in this study will be approximately 120 college freshmen and sophomores who are taking required introductory courses in the social and behavioral sciences at Doe University. Students are required to participate in a study of their choice from those listed by the department and receive course credit for their participation. Thus, the sample will not be randomly selected, which will limit the generalizability of the results. However, the fact that the courses are required for all students makes it likely that the sample will be diverse in terms of students' majors.

If you find you must propose using a sample of convenience, consider whether it will be possible to propose one that has *diversity*. For example, a proposal stating that students will be drawn from required courses at two or three colleges and universities (e.g., public, large private, and small liberal arts) will be stronger than one that relies on students at only a single institution. Likewise, if a researcher is going to propose approaching students on campus to interview them, a sample obtained at various times of the day and at diverse locations on campus would be stronger than one in which only students entering the cafeteria at lunchtime were sampled.

Note that for survey work in which the emphasis is on making sound generalizations to a population (such as a political poll of potential voters), proposing a convenience sample might doom the proposal. Convenience samples are more acceptable when researchers are conducting preliminary pilot studies of a phenomenon or when they were gathering preliminary data for theory building.

Exercise for Topic 29

1. Do you plan to use snowball sampling? If so, write a description of how you will sample.

2. Do you plan to use a sample of convenience? If so, write a description of how you will sample.

Other Methods of Sampling: II

If you are planning to study a population that is divided into a number of naturally existing groups with leaders, you might consider using *cluster sampling*. For instance, all students in a high school typically have a homeroom with a homeroom teacher (the leader). Rather than drawing individual names at random and then trying to contact individual students who will be scattered throughout the school, you might find it more convenient to draw a random sample of homerooms (i.e., clusters) and ask the homeroom teachers to gather the data for you (i.e., ask them to distribute questionnaires). Of course, you will want to draw a number of the homerooms. For instance, drawing only one homeroom with 30 students would not give you a good sample if it happened to be a homeroom for the academically talented. Example 1 shows how cluster sampling might be proposed.

Example 1

Cluster sampling will be used to obtain the sample for this study. Specifically, 20% of the homerooms ($n = 25$) in each of the four high schools in the school district will be selected at random. With administrative approval, the homeroom teachers will be asked to distribute and collect the completed questionnaires during the first homeroom period of the semester. Because the average class size in the district is 22, approximately 550 students will participate in the survey.[1]

---

[1] Note that *sample size* in this example is 25—not 550. For statistical reasons, the number of *units* selected at random determines the sample size.

The use of cluster sampling is not limited to school settings. It can be used for sampling from any population that is already separated into groups, such as Girl Scouts (who are in troops) and members of the Southern Baptist Convention (who are in congregations).

Multistage sampling is sometimes useful when sampling from a large population. For instance, suppose you want to sample registered nurses employed by hospitals in California. To use simple random sampling, you would need to get the names and contact information for all such nurses in order to give them all an equal chance when sampling (e.g., all their names must be in the hat). An alternative is to obtain a master list of all licensed hospitals in California and proceed as illustrated in Example 2.

Example 2

Multistage, stratified random sampling will be used to obtain the sample for this study. Specifically, the hospitals on a master list of all licensed hospitals in California will be divided into three groups: rural, urban, and suburban hospitals. From each group, 30% of the hospitals will be randomly selected. Appropriate administrators at each of the selected hospitals will be contacted by telephone to solicit their cooperation in identifying a random sample of 20% of the nurses they employ....

In Topics 27 through 30, we have considered various types of sampling plans that might be proposed. Typically, *how* you sample (e.g., at random) will be more important than *how many* you sample when your proposal is evaluated.

Nevertheless, you should propose sampling some specific number of participants—even if it is only a ballpark figure—in order to get feedback from your instructor. Topic 31 deals with the issue of sample size in more detail.

Exercise for Topic 30

1. Do you plan to use cluster sampling? If so, write a description of how you will sample.

2. Do you plan to use multistage sampling? If so, write a description of how you will sample.

Topic 31

Sample Size

When novice researchers begin planning their research, one of the questions that they often ask is, "How large does my sample have to be?" Unfortunately, there are no simple answers. In this topic, we will explore four practical considerations that bear on sample size.

First, review the literature you have collected to determine the typical sample size used in studies that are similar to yours. Pay particular attention to studies that employ the same method of research you are planning. For example, you will probably find that qualitative studies typically are based on much smaller samples than surveys.

Second, consider your resources. If you are a thesis or dissertation student with limited funds, even the cost of duplicating large numbers of questionnaires (let alone mailing costs) could be prohibitive if you propose studying a large sample. Likewise, conducting face-to-face interviews with large numbers of participants might be beyond your resources in terms of contacting them, interviewing them, and analyzing the large amount of data that would result.

Third, ask experienced researchers for their advice on the issue of sample size. For thesis and dissertation students, this is especially important. Ask the members of your committee what sample size they recommend given your purpose, method of research, and any other antici-

pated complexities you may face in conducting the research.

Fourth, keep in mind that you may be forgiven for using a sample that is smaller than typical for your type of research if you are proposing to explore research purposes, questions, or hypotheses that have great promise for advancing knowledge and are likely to have important implications. Put another way, proposing to use a very small sample to study a mundane research question might doom your proposal when it is evaluated by others. A proposal on a compelling research question might be approved even if you have the resources and contacts to obtain only a small sample.

Despite the above discussion, many students are likely to feel that they have been left out to dry on this topic without being given some specific numbers, so some will be offered here with the understanding that they are to be regarded as *exceedingly rough* guidelines for sample sizes that might be used in studies of different types.[1]

- For *qualitative research*, consider proposing an initial sample with 1 to 20 participants. Keep in mind that qualitative researchers sometimes adjust their sample size as they gather data and see the need for more participants or find that additional par-

---

[1] These are very rough, so this material should not be cited in a proposal to justify a particular sample size.

73

ticipants are not adding to the discovery of information.

- For *survey research* on very large populations, such as all citizens of a state, 800 or more participants might be proposed. (Professional pollsters often use 1,500.) For surveys of smaller populations, Table 1 near the end of this book provides suggested sample sizes that might be proposed.
- For *correlational research* and *test development research*, consider proposing to use 75 to 200 participants.
- For *experiments*, a sample size of 30 or less might be proposed if the administration of the treatments is time-consuming or expensive, or could potentially harm participants. Otherwise, 30 or more is desirable.

- For *causal-comparative research*, 30 or more might be proposed.
- The number for *program evaluation* will be determined largely by the number of program participants.

You may also remember from your statistics class that larger samples are more likely to yield statistically significant results than smaller samples. Thus, if you anticipate a small difference, which works against obtaining significance, consider proposing a large sample size to offset the small difference when you conduct significance tests.

Exercise for Topic 31

1. Examine the literature you have collected for use in your proposal. What is your estimate of the typical sample size used in published studies of the type you are planning?

2. Will you be proposing to use a sample size that is roughly the same as the one you named in response to Question 1? If not, what sample size will you propose? Explain.

Part G

Proposing Instrumentation

Under the major heading "Method," you should have described your proposed sample under the subheading "Participants." Next, you need a subheading for "Instrumentation," which will describe how you intend to measure the variables in your study. In this part of the book, you will learn how to write this section of the proposal.

The arrow in the outline in the following box shows where you are in the proposal-writing process.

```
        I.   Introduction
       II.   Literature Review*
      III.   Method
             A. Participants
             B. Instrumentation    ←You are here.
             C. Procedures
       IV.   Analysis
        V.   Discussion**
```

*May be integrated with the Introduction.
**Followed by writing a title and an abstract as well as developing
    a timeline.

Notes

Qualitative Instrumentation

Qualitative research is more free-form than quantitative research largely because qualitative researchers emphasize obtaining information from the point of view of the participants (see Topic 12). Highly structured instruments (i.e., objective measurement procedures) are incompatible with this goal because they impose a structure that is likely to influence how respondents perceive a phenomenon and respond to it. In other words, the act of measurement can influence respondents, and the more detailed and specific the instrument is, the more likely it is to influence them.

To avoid this problem, qualitative researchers often use open-ended interviews (i.e., questions are asked but respondents are not provided with choices to use as answers). Typically, these are *semistructured*, meaning that some questions will be developed in advance with follow-up questions developed on the spot in light of participants' responses. If you will be proposing to use such an instrument, be as specific as possible about its contents and use. The following example shows how this might be done.

Example

After reviewing relevant literature on immigrants' adjustment processes and the experiences of bicultural individuals, this writer will develop the interview questions. It is anticipated that there will be 10 sets of questions, each containing one general and several specific, open-ended questions, covering the following topics: (a) emigration and immigration experiences, (b) adjustment experiences im-

mediately after immigration, (c) family experiences, (d) cultural and social support, (e) Asian versus U.S. culture, (f) acculturation, (g) cultural identity, (h) ethnic identity, (i) biculturalism and bicultural competence, and (j) psychological support. For example, following is the set of questions for topic (b): "Please write about your experiences growing up in the U.S. How did you adjust to life in the U.S.? What difficulties did you experience? How did you learn English? How well did you think you fit into the U.S. society?"[1]

Of course, there can be many variations on this example. The main goal is to write a description that is as specific as possible while permitting you the flexibility that is desirable in qualitative research. Note that specificity may be required by instructors or funding agencies that will be evaluating your proposal.

Another measurement technique often used by qualitative researchers is direct observation either as a *participant observer* (one who is participating as a member of a group while making observations) or as a *nonparticipant observer* (one who is making observations but is not participating). If you will be proposing direct observation, consider addressing the following issues in your proposal: (a) the *types* of behaviors for which you will be observing, which should be determined by your research purposes, (b) who will make the observations, (c) when

---

[1] This example is based on the work of Kim, B. S. K., Brenner, B. R., Liang, C. T. H., & Asay, P. A. (2003). A qualitative study of adaptation experiences of 1.5-generation Asian Americans. *Cultural Diversity & Ethnic Minority Psychology, 9,* 156–170.

and where the observations will be made, (d) how the observations will be recorded, and (e) whether feedback on the first draft of the research report will be solicited from the participants. You should also address the issue of how long you will observe by discussing your *initial estimate*, which can be modified as needed while you are conducting the research.

Showing your readers that you have carefully considered your approach(es) to measurement in qualitative research will be a strength of your proposal.

Exercise for Topic 32

1. If you will be conducting qualitative research, will you be conducting interviews? Making observations? Using some other data-collection method?

2. Write a description of the instrumentation you will use.

Topic 33

Proposing Published Instruments

There are two types of *published instruments* in the social and behavioral sciences. First, there are tests and scales published by commercial publishers. Typically, these have undergone extensive development and much is known about their characteristics, such as their reliability and validity. Very often, they come with national norms that allow a comparison between the group you will be studying and a national norm group tested by the publisher.

Second, there are noncommercial published instruments. Usually, these are tests and scales that were developed by researchers for particular research purposes and are published in the sense that they appear in the journal articles reporting on their research or are available through test-collection services.[1]

Obviously, an important advantage of proposing to use published instruments is that others have gone to considerable trouble to develop and refine them. In your proposal, you can summarize what is already known about them to help justify their selection for use in your proposed study. The following example shows how this might be done.

Example

The Donovan Depression Scale (Donovan, 2000) will be used in this study. It has been widely used in other studies of depression, in-

cluding a number of recent studies (e.g., Doe, 2002; Johns, 2003; and Smith, 2004). Validity was established by the publisher by correlating the scale with other previously published measures of depression and anxiety. The correlations with the measures of depression were significantly higher than the correlations with anxiety, which is a pattern that is consistent with expectations. The test-retest reliability coefficient for this instrument was .79, indicating adequate reliability. Coefficient alpha is reported by the publisher to be .80, indicating adequate internal consistency. The use of this instrument in the proposed study will allow a direct comparison with the results of the numerous other studies in which this instrument has been used (see the literature review in this proposal).

The last sentence in this example is especially important. If you want to compare and contrast your results with those obtained in earlier research, you should consider proposing to use the same instrument(s) that were employed in that research. For instance, suppose you find that your treatment for depression is superior to one previously reported in the literature. If you use a *different* instrument, you will have confounded the comparison. That is, you will have used a different instrument and a different treatment from that previously used, so either could be the explanation for the observed difference in results.

The main reason for *not* using a published instrument is a possible mismatch between your research purposes, questions, or hypotheses and the available published instruments. For instance, sup-

---

[1] The ETS Test Collection is the largest in the world and includes an extensive library of 20,000 tests and other measurement devices from the early 1900s to the present. It can be accessed via the Internet at this address: http://www.ets.org/testcoll/index.html.

pose you want to measure a very limited number of algebra skills and all the available published tests cover much broader areas of algebra. In such a case, building a new test for the research would be appropriate. Information on proposing to write new instruments is provided in the next topic.

Exercise for Topic 33

Directions: If you will be using more than one published instrument, answer the following questions once for each instrument (e.g., answer the questions twice if you will be using two published instruments).

1. Will you be proposing to use a published instrument? If so, name it and give its source.

2. If you answered "yes" to Question 1, write a statement describing the proposed instrument, incorporating, if possible, information about its reliability and validity.

Proposing New Instruments

Near the end of the previous topic, you were advised that there should be a close match between your research purposes, questions, or hypotheses and the measuring instruments you propose to use. When there are no published instruments that match closely, you will need to develop new instruments.

When you are proposing to develop instruments for use in your research, it is usually insufficient to make a simple statement such as, "A new measure of parents' attitudes toward school will be developed." Instead, you should address the following issues: (1) why a new measure is needed, (2) what its underlying structure will be, that is, what broad areas will be covered, (3) what types of items will be used, and (4) how it will be developed and refined. The following example shows how this might be done.

Example

A measure of parents' attitudes toward their children's schools will be developed for use in this study. A new measure is needed because none of the existing scales address attitudes toward the unique aspects of the power structure in newly formed public charter schools, which is the primary focus of this proposed research. The new scale will cover three areas and have the following structure. First, there will be 10 items on the increased power and influence of parents in school decision making. Each item will consist of a statement that respondents will rate on a five-point scale from 5 (strongly agree) to 1 (strongly disagree). An illustrative item is: "Parents are too emotionally involved with their children to be good decision makers in setting school poli-

cies regarding discipline." Approximately 10 additional items of the same type will be on the increased power and influence of teachers in school decision making, and an additional 10 will be on the decreased power and influence of school principals.

An initial pool of 15 statements for each of the three areas will be brainstormed by three graduate students who have been active in the charter school movement. These statements will be reviewed by two professors who have experience in attitude-scale development and are knowledgeable of this movement. The pool of items will also be pilot-tested with a sample of five parents who will *not* be participants in the main study. Each parent will be asked to read each statement aloud and describe his or her reasons for selecting a choice from 5 to 1. This "think-aloud" technique will help to identify statements that parents find to be vague, ambiguous, or difficult to comprehend.

The final selection of 10 of the 15 statements for each area covered by the instrument will be made by the researcher in light of the feedback from the professors and the pilot test with parents.

Note that students planning research for their doctoral dissertation and those seeking major research funding may be expected to propose conducting full-scale reliability and validity studies on their new instruments before their use in the main study (see Topic 15). Also note that even for thesis research or research being proposed for a class project, the committee members or instructors who are reviewing the proposal may want to see at least a first draft of all the items before approving the proposal. Finally, note that showing in your proposal that a new instrument will be developed with care, including pilot testing and revision in light of feedback from others, will be a major strength of your research proposal.

Exercise for Topic 34

Directions: If you will be using more than one new instrument, answer the following question once for each instrument (e.g., answer the question twice if you will be using two new instruments).

1. Will you be developing a new instrument for use in your proposed research? If so, write a preliminary statement covering the four items listed in this topic. (See the numbered list of four items in the first column on the previous page.)

Topic 35
Proposing to Measure Demographics

In your section on instrumentation, you should address the issue of which demographics (i.e., background characteristics) you will measure. Demographic information will help to give your readers a picture of the participants in your research, and a statement regarding demographics should be included in proposals for both quantitative and qualitative research.

Keep in mind that some (if not many) participants might find demographic questions intrusive or objectionable, so it is best to ask for only those that are closely related to your research purposes, questions, or hypotheses. For example, a demographic question on religion would probably be inappropriate in a study on learning mathematics using manipulative materials.

Often in a proposal, it is adequate to make a simple statement that names the demographic variables. Example 1 shows such a statement.

Example 1
> Demographic information on gender, age, ethnicity, and highest level of education completed will be collected.

If you are expected to be more specific about how you will collect demographic information, provide more details, as illustrated in Example 2.

Example 2
> The last section of the questionnaire will request demographic information on gender, age, ethnicity, and highest level of education completed. This section will be clearly marked as "optional," with a statement to the effect that it is needed for statistical purposes and will help the researchers to understand more about the participants. Because age is potentially sensitive among this group of adults, ages will be presented in grouped intervals (e.g., 18–29, 30–39) so that participants will not be asked to indicate their specific ages. Ethnicity is also potentially sensitive and poses problems in wording (e.g., Latina vs. Chicana). Thus, the question for this variable will be open-ended without choices, which will allow participants to use terms of their own choice when responding to this item.[1]

When using children as participants, consider whether it is appropriate to ask them for the demographic information you desire. Young children may not be valid sources of information on variables such as ethnicity, household income, and religion. In addition, it might be unethical and insensitive to collect this information from children without their parents' permission. In your proposal, you should address how you will collect such information about the children. For instance, teachers might be asked for information on the children's ethnicity. Whatever manner you plan to use to collect such information, spell it out in your proposal.

---

[1] For more information on collecting information on sensitive demographic variables, including the use of choices for soliciting information on race/ethnicity, see Patten, M. L. (2001). *Questionnaire research: A practical guide* (2nd ed.). Los Angeles: Pyrczak Publishing.

Exercise for Topic 35

1. What types of demographic information do you plan to collect?

2. Write a brief statement naming the demographic variables (see Example 1 in this topic).

3. If you are expected to write a more detailed statement regarding demographics, write it below (see Example 2 in this topic).

Ethical Issues in Measurement

Measuring in order to gather data for research purposes often raises ethical issues. When this is the case, you should explicitly address the matter in your proposal.

First, you should plan to protect your participants' *privacy*. By collecting *anonymous* responses to questionnaires and other instruments, you can provide them with this protection. Thus, if you will be providing anonymity, you should state that in your proposal.

Sometimes, having the participants remain anonymous will not be possible. First, you may need to know their identities in order to match them with other sources of information. For example, to achieve your research purpose, you might need to match individual participants' responses to an instrument with their GPAs on school records. In addition, some measurement techniques are inherently not anonymous, such as face-to-face interviews or direct observation of behavior. When this is the case, the best you can offer is *confidentiality*, that is, sharing the information you collect with only those who need to know it in order to conduct the research. The following example shows how this issue might be addressed in a research proposal.

Example

Because it will be necessary to match individual participants' scores on this measure of risk-taking tendencies with the information on their safety record contained in their personnel files, participants will be asked to write their names on the answer sheets. However, they will be advised that the information will remain confidential. To assure that this is the case, the answer sheets will be collected by this researcher and kept in a secure location until the safety-record information from the personnel files has been recorded on the answer sheets by the researcher. Once this is done, the researcher will physically remove (cut out) the names of the respondents and archive the answer sheets in a secure location.

As you plan your instrumentation, you should also consider how to provide *protection from psychological harm*. Suppose you plan to interview women who recently survived a rape experience. Because the interview may cause trauma, you should inform them in advance of the topic of the interview, obtain their consent, and assure them that they are free to withdraw from the interview at any time without penalty. Some researchers investigating such sensitive matters have even made available psychological counseling on a 24-hour basis for a limited amount of time (such as for a week after the data collection) in order to help participants who were unintentionally harmed by participation in the research.

Sometimes, the potential for harm may be subtle. For instance, you might need to administer an attitude-toward-math scale to third graders. If you do this during classroom time, you might be depriving the students of other instructional activities that will benefit them directly. (Most research benefits participants only very indirectly.) Even if you consider this a minor matter, the school officials from whom you will need to get permission to conduct the research might view it differently and deny you access.

Most universities and other research institutions and agencies require that research proposals be reviewed by a committee that will consider the issues covered in this topic. This committee is likely to pay special attention to what you will be measuring and how you will be measuring it, with an eye to whether participants are adequately protected.

Note that review committees are usually also responsible for reviewing the informed-consent form (a printed expla-nation of the research for potential respondents), so you should obtain a copy of your institution's guidelines on preparing such a form early in the research planning process.

The next section of this book deals with research procedures you will propose. Because these can also harm participants, ethical issues will be considered again in Topic 39.

Exercise for Topic 36

1. Do you anticipate that your measurement procedures will raise any ethical issues? Explain.

2. If you answered "yes" to Question 1, write a description that explicitly addresses the issues, including how you propose to minimize them.

Part H

Proposing Procedures

Under the major heading "Method," you should have described your proposed sample under the subheading "Participants" and your measurement techniques under the subheading "Instrumentation." The last subheading under "Method" typically is "Procedures." Under this subheading, you should describe any physical acts you will perform to execute the research.

The arrow in the outline in the following box shows where you are in the proposal-writing process.

```
     I.  Introduction
    II.  Literature Review*
   III.  Method
         A. Participants
         B. Instrumentation
         C. Procedures          ←You are here.
    IV.  Analysis
     V.  Discussion**
```

*May be integrated with the Introduction.
**Followed by writing a title and an abstract as well as developing a timeline.

Notes

Topic 37

Nonexperimental Procedures

In the "Procedures" subsection, you should describe the physical things you plan to do in order to conduct your study. Usually, you should address these issues: what you will do, when you will do it, and for how long you will do it.[1] This should be done even for seemingly simple methodological studies such as mailed surveys, which is illustrated in Example 1.

Example 1

Postcards that describe the upcoming study will be mailed to all names on the mailing list. These cards will stress the importance of the study and ask recipients to watch their mail for the questionnaire that will be arriving soon. Previous research indicates that prior notification by postcard has a positive effect on response rate (Doe, 2004).

One week after the postcards are mailed, the questionnaires with a cover letter and stamped envelope will be mailed. Two weeks later, all potential respondents will be mailed a second copy of the questionnaire and envelope with a cover letter that stresses the importance of the study and asks them to ignore the second mailing if they have already responded to the first one.

The postcard, cover letters, and questionnaire will be reviewed by all members of the thesis committee and revised, if necessary, prior to mailing.

If participants will be physically present while you gather the data, you should describe the location, what will be done in their presence, and how long the interaction is anticipated to last. Example 2 is the proposed procedure for an observational study of mother-child communication.

Example 2

When each mother-child dyad arrives at the Child Development Laboratory, they will be taken by the researcher to a private room, and the mother and child will be asked to take a seat at a small table. At that point, a beeper will go off, and the researcher will state that she is needed in another part of the laboratory but will return shortly. Before leaving the room, she will remove the Lollipop Puzzle (described below) from a drawer and offer it to the child to play with while waiting for the researcher to return. After leaving the room, the researcher will then observe the mother and child through a one-way mirror and record relevant aspects of their communication on the Communicative Dissonance Direct Observation Checklist described under Instrumentation. At the end of the 10-minute observation period, the researcher will return to the room, praise the child for making progress in putting the puzzle together, and....

It is usually desirable to propose that procedures such as those in Example 2 will be pilot-tested and revised as needed before being used in the main study. In a pilot study, for example, you might learn that the task you plan to provide (the puzzle) does not stimulate sufficient mother-child communication for you to gather the data you need or that 10 minutes is too long or too short a period for the task.

Providing detailed information on procedures will allow a proper evaluation of your proposal.

---

[1] Qualitative researchers should describe *anticipated* procedures because they might modify them during the course of their research.

Exercise for Topic 37

1. Write a detailed description of your procedures, have it reviewed by others, and revise it. (If you will be conducting an *experiment*, you should wait until after you have read Topic 38 to write the description.)

Procedures in Experiments

A classic, simple experiment consists of two groups that are given different treatments. Your first obligation under "Procedures" is to describe how individuals will arrive at their group membership. If they will be assigned at random to groups, which is highly desirable, you should explicitly say so. On the other hand, if they are already in groups (such as students already enrolled in one high school to be compared with those enrolled in another one), this should be stated and any information on their comparability should be provided. For instance, are the achievement levels at the two high schools comparable? Do the students in the two schools come from similar socioeconomic levels?

If you will not be using random assignment to groups, it is good to acknowledge that this will not be done, then follow with a statement on why you are not proposing it. Often, this is because you do not have sufficient control over or cooperation from participants.

Your next obligation is to describe in as much detail as possible what will be done to the experimental group. For very complex treatments, such as a year-long new curriculum program in first-grade mathematics, you might describe it in sufficient detail so that your readers can visualize the *types* of things that will be done and refer them to a published source (such as a curriculum guide) for details on day-to-day activities. An alternative

for very complex treatments is to once again describe the *types* of things that will be done and prepare a detailed appendix on the treatment to include at the end of your proposal. The following example, which is only a partial description of an experimental treatment, illustrates the level of detail that might be desirable in a proposal for an experiment.

Example

Each member of the experimental group will be seated at a computer console. The computer program will present two simulated robberies, lasting about three minutes each. Each participant will be shown a robbery committed by a member of her or his own race (e.g., a white participant will view a white robber). Then, each participant will view a robbery committed by a member of a different race (e.g., a white participant will view a robbery committed by an African American). After a five-minute break, participants will be asked to view simulated police lineups and to rate each individual in the lineups in terms of....

Next, you should describe what will be done to the control or comparison group. Note that whatever happens to them during the course of the experiment will be important for interpreting the resulting data.

Sometimes experiments are conducted using a single group. For example, a group might receive normal praise for a while, then increased praise, followed by the reintroduction of normal praise. When proposing such an experiment, state how long each condition is expected to last and specifically what will be done in each.

Because the purpose of an experiment is to determine the effects of *treat-ments* on some outcome measure(s), a detailed description of the treatments is essential in a good proposal for experimental research.

Exercise for Topic 38

1. If you will be conducting an experiment, write a first draft of the description of the experimental treatment.

2. Write a description of what will be done to the control group while the experimental group is receiving its treatment.

3. Do you anticipate referring your readers to published sources for more information on the treatment(s)? Do you anticipate including an appendix with detailed information on the treatment(s)? Explain.

Topic 39

Ethical Issues and Procedures

Topic 36 pointed out that the act of measurement may pose ethical problems if participants' rights to *privacy* are not adequately protected. In addition, the act of measurement might cause *psychological* harm and stress.

Likewise, the procedures used in research might cause psychological harm. For example, suppose a confederate (someone working for you as a researcher) is going to fake a physical assault on another confederate while the true participants in the study are onlookers. Your goal is to determine the extent to which the participants will intervene to stop the assault. As you can imagine, merely witnessing such an assault might be quite disturbing. In addition, if participants fail to intervene, they will gain insights about themselves that may cause self-doubt due to their inaction. To complicate matters, this study also holds the potential for *physical harm* because some participants might physically intervene and get hurt in the process.

Sometimes, research projects that clearly have the potential for psychological and physical harm are ethically conducted *if* the participants were fully informed of the nature of the research and the potential for harm and freely agreed to participate. However, for the study we are considering above, if potential participants are informed that the physical attack will be a fake attack, the experiment would lose its validity. As a general

rule, novice researchers should avoid proposing such highly problematic research projects.

To complicate matters, the potential for harm can be subtle and difficult to predict in advance. For instance, recently a researcher proposed lightly brushing just inside students' nostrils with a cotton swab in order to obtain sample cultures. One member of the university's institutional review board raised the obvious concern that the person using the swabs might not be properly trained, insert it too far, and harm the participants. Another member of the board raised the somewhat less obvious issue of sterility. Could the researcher assure the committee that the swabs would be sterile? Even if they are, participants might *perceive* that they were not. For instance, a participant who came down with the flu the day after the study might accuse the researcher of giving the flu to him or her. After discussing these issues, the committee recommended that the cultures be collected by a registered nurse, who would have specialized knowledge and skills useful in protecting the participants. The proposal was rewritten to include the use of a registered nurse and then approved by the committee.

The example we have just considered illustrates the value of institutional review boards in helping to protect participants. Before submitting your proposal to such a committee, try to brainstorm with others about what types of things might go wrong. Then, address them explicitly in your proposal—with attention to measures you will take to help protect the participants.

Exercise for Topic 39

1. Are you aware of any potential psychological harm your procedures might pose? Explain.

2. Are you aware of any potential physical harm your procedures might pose? Explain.

3. If you answered "yes" to Question 1 and/or Question 2, write a statement addressing the possible harm for inclusion in the "Procedures" subsection of your proposal.

Part I

Proposing Methods of Analysis

Your next step is to propose a method of analysis. This part of the book starts with some guidelines for analyzing qualitative data. Then, statistical methods are considered. The statistics in this part of the book are limited to those commonly taught in an introductory statistics class.

Important Notes

In this part, Topic 40 deals with qualitative analysis. Topics 41 through 44 cover ways to analyze data quantitatively and should be read in sequence because some of the statistical terms defined in earlier topics are *not* redefined in later ones.

Unless you are thoroughly grounded in basic statistical methods, you may find some of the material in Topics 41 through 44 difficult to follow. If you are in this situation, consider either taking more coursework in statistics or locating a statistics tutor or consultant to assist you in writing your proposed method of analysis. Note that having a fuzzy or unsuitable proposed method of analyzing data can be a fatal flaw in a research proposal.

```
        I.   Introduction
       II.   Literature Review*
      III.   Method
              A. Participants
              B. Instrumentation
              C. Procedures
       IV.   Analysis          ←You are here.
        V.   Discussion**
```

*May be integrated with the Introduction.
**Followed by writing a title and an abstract as well as developing
  a timeline.

Notes

Topic 40

Qualitative Analysis

Careful, systematic plans for the analysis of qualitative data distinguish serious qualitative scholars from those who confuse qualitative research with casual everyday observation.

Typically, the proposed method of analysis should describe which method(s) of analysis will be employed and the major steps that will be followed. Example 1 illustrates how this might be briefly done.

Example 1[1]

Hill et al.'s (1997) consensual qualitative research (CQR) specifies a series of procedures to code the data across participant responses. First, the primary research team will take the following two steps for each case (i.e., participant data): (a) Assign chunks of data to domains (or themes) and (b) develop abstracts within domains based on core ideas (i.e., essence of participant responses). In each step, the primary team members initially will complete the tasks independently and work together to develop a consensus version of the product (i.e., one that is agreeable to everyone in the research team). Then, an auditor who *will not be involved in the previous procedure* will examine the domains and core ideas to ensure that the data were accurately represented. Any inaccuracies identified by the auditor will be reconsidered by the primary team for possible changes. Following the audit, the primary research team will take the following two steps: (a) Identify categories (i.e., clusters of core ideas across cases) based on core ideas in each domain and (b) determine the frequency of categories across cases.

Again, the primary research team will initially work independently and then work together to form consensus products in each of the two steps, and the auditor will examine the categories and their frequency to verify their accuracy. Finally, to verify that all domains, core ideas, and categories have been identified, the primary team will conduct a stability check using data from the remaining two cases.

Notice that in Example 1, more than one person will be involved in the analysis. If you have the contacts and resources to have other individuals assist in the analysis, it is recommended that you propose to do so.

In the original report in which Example 1 appeared, the material in the example was labeled as an overview. This was followed by explication of the specifics of each major step in the analysis. Example 2 shows how this was done for one of the steps.

Example 2

Primary research team members will *independently review the core ideas for potential similarities across cases,* which will lead to a higher level of abstraction of the data. When similarities across cases are noted, the members will create a category that best represents the observed similarity. The primary team will then work together to develop a consensus version of the categories. Then, one of three labels will be applied to each category to describe the frequency of its occurrence. *General* will be applied to categories that occur in all cases (i.e., all participants). *Typical* will be used to describe categories that occur in half or more cases, and *Variant* will be applied to categories that are found to occur in less than half of the cases.

---

[1] Examples 1 and 2 are based on the work of Kim, B. S. K., Brenner, B. R., Liang, C. T. H., & Asay, P. A. (2003). A qualitative study of adaptation experiences of 1.5-generation Asian Americans. *Cultural Diversity & Ethnic Minority Psychology, 9,* 156–170.

When possible, it is also a good idea to propose "member checking," in which participants are asked to review the results and provide feedback to the researcher on their accuracy.

Exercise for Topic 40

1. If you will be conducting qualitative analysis, will you have other researchers help (or supervise) you during the analysis? Will you use an auditor? Explain.

2. Write a proposal for the analysis of your qualitative data. (Consider preparing a step-by-step description as illustrated by the examples in this topic.)

Topic 41

Analysis of Demographics

In Topic 35, you were urged to collect data on the participants' demographics (i.e., their background characteristics). Whether your proposed research is qualitative or quantitative, you should state in your proposal how you will analyze this data.

Many demographics are measured at what is known as the *nominal level of measurement*. At this level, participants were put into categories that have word names (as opposed to scores). For instance, gender is a nominal variable with the categories (in words) of "males" and "females." Likewise, political affiliation is a nominal variable with categories such as "Republican," "Democrat," "Reform," and "Independent."

Many other demographics are measured at the *equal interval level* (known as *interval* and *ratio levels* in statistics classes).[1] At this level, participants are classified on a numerical scale in which all score points are equally distant from each other. For example, *age* is measured at the equal interval level because the difference between any points on the scale (such as the difference between 2 years and 3 years) is the same as the distance between any other two points (such as the difference between 20 years and 21 years). Other common demo-

graphics measured at this level are household income (measured in dollars), years of education completed, and number of children. Likewise, scores obtained using objective tests are usually assumed to be equal interval.

Often, demographics at both the nominal and equal interval levels will be measured in the same study. The following example shows a proposed analysis for this situation.

Example

For the demographic data for variables measured at the nominal level (gender and ethnicity), percentages will be computed and reported along with the numbers of cases in each category. For equal interval data (age and number of years abusing drugs), means and standard deviations will be computed. If the distributions for either of these variables are highly skewed, medians and interquartile ranges will also be computed and reported.

If you have two or more distinct groups in your study, such as participants who abuse marijuana and participants who abuse heroin, you could propose to report their demographics separately. For instance, you could add the words "separately for each of the two groups in this study" immediately after the word "category" at the end of the first sentence in the example.

Sometimes, scores are grouped when demographics are measured. For instance, income might be measured by having participants check off the income group (e.g., $0–$9,999; $10,000–$19,000; etc.) to which they belong.

---

[1] You may recall from your statistics class that the *ordinal* level of measurement puts participants in rank order. This level of measurement is seldom used in collection of demographic data. Should you have such data, consider proposing the calculation of medians and interquartile ranges.

These groups are known as *score intervals*. For such data, you should propose to calculate the percentage for each income interval and report the percentages with the numbers of cases in each interval.

If some of the terminology in this section is only vaguely familiar to you, consult your statistics textbook to refresh your memory. If you need a quick, non-technical review of introductory statistics, *Making Sense of Statistics: A Conceptual Overview* by Fred Pyrczak (Los Angeles: Pyrczak Publishing) is recommended.

Note that it is not usually necessary to name the computer program you will be using or to show the formulas to be used *unless* you are required to do so for instructional purposes.

Exercise for Topic 41

1. Which demographic variables, if any, will you be measuring at the nominal level?

2. Which demographic variables, if any, will you be measuring at the equal interval level (either interval or ratio scales)?

3. Write a first draft of a paragraph in which you propose the analysis of the demographic data you will be collecting.

Topic 42

Relationships: Nominal

Often, a research purpose, question, or hypothesis requires the examination of relationships between nominal variables. Nominal variables are those that put participants into "named" categories, such as the variable called gender, which puts participants into the categories "male" and "female." Example 1 shows a research purpose concerning the relationship between two nominal variables: gender (male vs. female) and completion (completed vs. not completed).

Example 1
This study will examine the relationship between gender and successful completion of a behavioral drug rehabilitation program.

Example 2 shows a proposed method of analysis for the research question in Example 1.

Example 2
To examine the relationship between gender and successful completion of the behavioral drug rehabilitation program, a two-way contingency table with percentages and numbers of cases shown in each cell will be prepared. The statistical significance of the differences in the table will be tested at the .05 level with a chi-square test.[1]

In Example 2, the term *two-way contingency table* is used. In case you have forgotten what this is, Example 3 shows one with some hypothetical data.

Example 3

	Program completed	Program not completed
Male	33.3% ($n = 10$)	66.7% ($n = 20$)
Female	66.7% ($n = 20$)	33.3% ($n = 10$)

Note the use of the phrase "at the .05 level" in Example 2. This means that if the probability that the relationship would be created by random error is 5 in 100 *or less*, the relationship will be declared statistically significant. The .05 level is the most common one used in research proposals.

The *chi-square test* is designed for use when determining the significance of the relationship between two nominal variables. Of course, more than one relationship can be examined in a proposed study. Frequently, researchers have a key variable such as gender that will be related to a number of other variables such as (a) gender and program completion, (b) gender and returning for a follow-up examination, (c) gender and becoming employed, and so on.

Also note that each nominal variable can have more than two categories. Example 4 on the next page shows a contingency table for a variable in which one variable (experience) has three categories. The relationship between the two variables in this table should also be tested for significance with a chi-square test.

---

[1] The chi-square test will determine only whether the relationship is statistically significant. To describe the strength of the relationship, you might propose to calculate a coefficient of contingency or Cramér's statistic (ϕ').

Example 4

	Highly experienced	Somewhat experienced	Not at all experienced
Male	25.0% ($n = 100$)	25.0% ($n = 100$)	50.0% ($n = 200$)
Female	44.4% ($n = 40$)	33.3% ($n = 30$)	22.2% ($n = 20$)

In the next topic, analysis of the relationship between two equal interval (i.e., interval and ratio) variables is considered.

Exercise for Topic 42

1. If you will be examining the relationship between nominal variables, write a first draft of your proposed analysis here:

Topic 43
Relationships: Equal Interval

Often, a research purpose, question, or hypothesis requires the examination of the relationship between two equal interval (i.e., interval or ratio) variables.[1] Following are some examples of research questions that do this.

- To what extent do reading-readiness test scores obtained in kindergarten predict reading-achievement test scores obtained at the end of first grade?

- How strongly correlated are job satisfaction and compensation?

- Are College Board SAT scores or high school GPAs a better predictor of college freshmen GPAs?

Note that the last research question requires that two relationships be examined: (1) the relationship between SAT scores and college GPA and (2) the relationship between high school GPA and college GPA. The variable with the stronger relationship with college GPA is the better predictor.

The standard statistic for examining relationships between two equal interval measures is the Pearson product-moment correlation coefficient. You may recall that its symbol is r and that it ranges from -1.00 (perfect inverse relationship) through 0.00 (no relationship) to 1.00 (perfect direct relationship).

The following example shows how the analysis might be proposed for a study with two equal interval variables.

Example

First, the distributions on the Doe Depression Scale and the Smith Manifest Anxiety Scale will be examined. Based on the literature on these measures when used with samples of college students, it is assumed that there will be considerable variation in both distributions and that neither will be significantly skewed. If these assumptions are correct, the analysis will proceed as follows. First, means and standard deviations will be computed as measures of central tendency and variability, respectively. Then, a Pearson product-moment correlation coefficient will be computed for the relationship between the scores on the two measures. The resulting correlation coefficient will be tested for statistical significance at the .05 level. If it is significant, the value of the coefficient of determination (r^2) will be computed to aid in interpreting the magnitude of the relationship.

If you wish to determine how well one variable can be predicted from a *combination* of other variables (such as predicting college GPA from high school GPA *and* SAT scores), you should propose to conduct a multiple linear regression, which will yield a value of R (i.e., the multiple correlation coefficient). Like r, it can range from -1.00 to 1.00.

While you will be able to conduct and interpret simple correlational studies based on what you learned in an introductory statistics class, for more advanced methods, you will need a course in advanced correlational techniques.

---

[1] Note that most physical measurements, as well as scores on objective tests and scales, are assumed to be equal interval.

Exercise for Topic 43

1. Do you anticipate proposing to use correlational techniques? If so, which variables will be correlated with each other?

2. If you will be conducting a correlational study, write a first draft of your proposed method of analysis.

Topic 44

Group Differences

Often, a research purpose, question, or hypothesis requires examination of the relationship between a nominal variable and an equal interval variable. Here is an example of a research question that does this:

• Is individual competition for prizes or participation in cooperative learning groups more effective in promoting achievement in first-grade mathematics? (Note: Placement in either an individual competition condition or in a cooperative learning condition is a *nominal* variable. Mathematics achievement is usually measured with an objective test, which is assumed to be *equal interval*.)

To examine the relationship between the two variables we are considering, the usual method of analysis is based on a comparison of *average group differences*. That is, if there is a difference between the averages of the two groups on a mathematics test, then there is a relationship between how they were treated (individual competition vs. cooperative learning) and their achievement test scores in mathematics. Example 1 illustrates a proposed method of analysis for this situation.

Example 1
    Assuming that the distribution of scores is not significantly skewed, the analysis will proceed as follows. First, for each student, a change score will be computed by subtracting the pretest score from the posttest score. Then, means and standard deviations will be computed

separately for pretest, posttest, and change scores for each group. Finally, the significance of the difference between the two mean change scores will be determined at the .05 level with a two-tailed t test for independent groups.

Example 1 is based on an experiment with a pretest and a posttest. The relationship between a nominal variable and an equal interval variable can also be examined in a nonexperimental study, as illustrated by this research purpose:

• The purpose of this research is to compare the trust in authority reported by three groups of teenage boys: (1) those who were physically abused, (2) those who were sexually abused, and (3) those who were not abused. Trust in authority will be measured with an objective self-report measure developed by Doe (2004).

The nominal variable (abuse) has three categories (physical, sexual, and no-abuse), so the analysis will require the computation of three means and standard deviations, as indicated in Example 2. Note that trust was measured only once (not as a pretest followed by a posttest).

Example 2
    Assuming that the distribution of scores is not significantly skewed, the analysis will proceed as follows. First, the means and standard deviations of the trust scores will be computed for the three groups of boys. The differences among the three means will be tested with a one-way ANOVA with p set at .05. If this is statistically significant, individual pairs of

means will be tested for significance using
Scheffé's test (a multiple comparisons test).

Exercise for Topic 44

1. Will you be examining differences among groups? If so, name the groups.

2. Will there be pretests and posttests *or* only one test for each participant?

3. If you will be measuring one or more nominal variables (to form groups) and comparing equal interval measurements for the groups, write a proposed method of analysis here.

Part J

Concluding Tasks

After you have proposed a method of analysis for the data you plan to collect, you should wrap up the proposal with a discussion section, give the proposal a title, prepare an abstract of the proposal, develop a timeline, and have the first draft of your proposal reviewed. These tasks are discussed in this part of the book.

```
      I.   Introduction
     II.   Literature Review*
    III.   Method
            A. Participants
            B. Instrumentation
            C. Procedures
     IV.   Analysis
      V.   Discussion**          ←You are here.
```

    *May be integrated with the Introduction.
   **Followed by writing a title and an abstract as well as developing
    a timeline.

Notes

Topic 45

Writing a Discussion Section

The body of a research proposal should end with a discussion section. Consider beginning this section with a *summary* of the material that preceded it. While it may seem redundant to do this, keep in mind that many readers read quickly and may have skipped over important ideas (and this is your chance to present them again). Other readers may have lost the big picture while considering the details (and this is your chance to help them refocus). If you write a summary, emphasize why your problem area is important and how your particular research purposes, questions, or hypotheses will help to advance knowledge of the problem area in which you are proposing to work.

After the summary part of the discussion, consider discussing the *limitations* of the research methodology. For example, are you proposing to use a limited sample, or do you know of certain flaws in your instruments? Generally, it is best to acknowledge these explicitly so that your readers will know that you are aware of what is ideal but are working under real-life constraints. Example 1 shows part of a discussion of limitations.

Example 1

There are several limitations to this study. The sample will consist of rural families who live near a college town. The findings, therefore, will be generalizable only to such families. Another limitation is that the sample will be contacted through child care facilities. Thus, the results will not apply to families who do not use child care. Finally, due to limited re-

sources, the semistructured interviews will be conducted via telephone. Face-to-face interviews would be more desirable than telephone interviews in order to establish rapport with the participants and to observe their reactions while they answer the questions.

In addition, if you will be conducting an experiment and will not be able to assign participants at random to experimental and control conditions, it is important to acknowledge this limitation.

Consider ending the discussion section with a statement regarding the possible *implications*. Typically, implications address how individuals and organizations will be able to use the results by answering questions such as: Will the results help professionals to better understand the phenomena that you plan to investigate? Will they help them to formulate better theories? Will they help them to provide better services to their clients and students? Example 2 shows part of such a discussion.

Example 2

Despite the limitations noted above, this study will provide the first test of the Doe's Grief Therapy Model in a sample of Hispanic women. As such, it will help therapists to understand the applicability of the model for working with such individuals when they are grieving the loss of a significant other. In addition, this study will provide insights into....

A detailed statement regarding possible implications is a strong way to end a proposal.

Exercise for Topic 45

1. Will you begin the discussion section with a summary? If so, write a first draft of it.

2. Will you discuss the methodological limitations of your study? If so, write a first draft of your discussion.

3. Write a first draft of a discussion of possible implications of your study.

Topic 46

Giving the Proposal a Title

Writing a title should be done with care because it is the first element that most readers will consider when reviewing your proposal.

One of the most important principles in writing a title is to avoid the temptation to be clever. Engaging in empirical research is a serious matter, and your proposal deserves a serious title.

When writing the title, reexamine your research purposes, questions, or hypotheses to identify the main variables. These should be referred to in the title. Example 1 shows a research purpose and a corresponding title.

Example 1

Research purpose: To explore the relationship between self-reported altruism and the decision to donate one's organs.

Corresponding title: An Investigation of the Relationship Between Altruism and the Decision to Make Organ Donations

Notice that the title is *not* a sentence and does *not* end with a period. These are appropriate characteristics of a title for empirical research.

If there are many variables in your purpose, question, or hypothesis, consider referring to them by *type*. For instance, if you are proposing to study 12 personality variables as they are exhibited by high-achieving women in sociology, refer to "personality traits" in the title instead of naming all 12 variables, as is done in Example 2.

Example 2

Personality Traits of High-Achieving Women in Sociology: A Research Proposal

Notice that Example 2 ends with the subtitle "A Research Proposal," which could be added to any main title unless your title page already has this phrase on it elsewhere.

For an experiment or causal-comparative study, the usual form for a title is "The Effects of A on B" or "The Effectiveness of A in Producing Changes in B," or "The Influence of A on B." Example 3 contains two titles. The first one is for an experiment, and the second one is for a causal-comparative study.

Example 3

The Effects of Computer-Assisted Instruction on the Mathematics Achievement of Low-Achieving Second Grade Students

The Influence of Birth Order on the Development of Psychomotor Skills Among Children

Finally, avoid referring to anticipated results in the title. While you may discuss the anticipated results when you introduce a hypothesis in a proposal, results seldom belong in the title. Example 4 illustrates this.

Example 4

Poor title because it states anticipated results: Welfare Mothers Trained with the Wisconsin Program Should be More Employable Than Control Mothers

Improved title: The Effects of the Wisconsin Program on the Employability of Welfare Mothers

Exercise for Topic 46

1. Write a tentative title for your research proposal, following the guidelines in this topic.

Topic 47

Preparing an Abstract

An abstract is a summary that provides an overview of the proposal. When there are many competing proposals (such as for research funding), preparing a good abstract is exceedingly important because some reviewers may make a first pass and eliminate certain proposals based on the abstract alone. For instance, if the funding agency is concentrating on inner-city adolescents and your abstract fails to mention this group, it may not get further consideration.

For many academic purposes (such as a term project), a short abstract (say, 150–200 words) is adequate. You should check your institution's or instructor's requirements regarding length. If you find that you are required to write a very short abstract, consider limiting yourself to these topics:

- Research purposes, questions, or hypotheses
- Relationship to the literature
- The type of research being proposed (e.g., survey, qualitative, and so on)
- Types of implications that might result from the findings

Example 1 covers these elements in a short abstract.

Example 1
The purpose of the proposed research is to examine purchasing patterns of college freshmen using the Internet. This topic is especially timely because the literature indicates that in each of the past 10 years, spending on Internet purchases by young adults has increased dramatically. A mailed survey will be used to collect data on the frequency with which purchases are made, the types of items purchased, and the reasons for shopping on the Internet instead of shopping through more traditional channels. The results of this research will have implications for consumer educators who teach consumer economics as well as those who prepare curricula for consumer economics courses.

Note that in the short abstract in Example 1, details on sampling, measurement, and methods of analysis are omitted. If a long abstract is required or permitted, these elements may be covered. For longer abstracts, consider using subheadings to guide readers. Example 2 shows a typical set of subheadings that might be used within an abstract.

Example 2
Problem area (including importance)
Research purpose (or question or hypothesis)
Related literature (brief overview of most salient aspects)
Participants (including sampling plan)
Instrumentation (types of instruments that will be used; names of instruments are usually not needed in the abstract)
Method of analysis (descriptive and inferential, if any, *or* type of qualitative analysis)
Potential implications

If you are writing a long abstract, be careful that it does not become so long that it is a burden to someone who is examining it only to obtain an overview of your proposed research.

Exercise for Topic 47

1. Are you required to write a short abstract? If so, how many words are permitted?

2. Will you be writing a long abstract? If so, will you be using subheadings?

3. Write the first draft of an abstract for your proposal.

Topic 48

Developing a Timeline

Many novice researchers seriously underestimate the amount of time that it will take them to conduct and write their research. Thus, it is important to draw up a timeline and seek feedback on it from experienced researchers.

All researchers should build into their timelines adequate time for others to review their work as it progresses. Thesis and dissertation students should also consult with their chair regarding whether the chair wants to review all written materials *before* other committee members are given copies. If so, additional time will be needed to allow for a two-stage review of each part of the research report.

Example 1 shows a sample timeline submitted by one student. Keep in mind that timelines can vary dramatically depending on the circumstances of the research. For instance, in this case, the student prepared a preliminary literature review for the proposal and will need to complete it. Other students may have written a complete literature review while preparing their proposals. Also, this student was employed full-time and could devote only evenings and weekends to conducting the research.

Example 1
1. Complete literature review. (one month)
2. Have literature review reviewed by the thesis chair. (two weeks) Have literature review reviewed by other committee members. (two more weeks)
3. Obtain mailing lists from University Data Center. (two weeks)

4. Prepare survey cover letter and first draft of questionnaire. (one week)
5. Have cover letter and questionnaire reviewed by committee chair. (one week)
6. Pilot test cover letter and questionnaire, and revise. (one week)
7. Have revised cover letter and questionnaire reviewed by thesis chair. (two weeks) Have them reviewed by other committee members. (two more weeks)
8. Write the Method section of the research report. (two weeks)
9. Have the Method section reviewed by the thesis chair. (two weeks) Have it reviewed by other committee members. (two more weeks)
10. Mail letter and questionnaire, and wait for responses. (three weeks)
11. Mail follow-up questionnaire, and wait for responses. (two weeks)
12. Tabulate responses. Conduct descriptive and inferential analyses. (two weeks)
13. Write the Results and Discussion sections of the research report. (two weeks)
14. Have the Results and Discussion sections reviewed by the thesis chair. (two weeks) Have them reviewed by other committee members. (two more weeks)
15. Assemble the first draft of the complete report. Have it reviewed by an instructor at the University Writing Center for mechanical flaws in grammar, punctuation, etc. (one week)
16. Submit the complete first draft (revised in light of Step 15) to the committee chair and the committee members for their review. (two weeks)
17. Rewrite and revise in light of Step 16, and resubmit for feedback. (two weeks)
18. Make final changes based on Step 17. (one week)
19. Format the thesis and submit it to the University Librarian for format approval. (one week)

20.   Take a vacation in Hawaii!

If you have sufficient time, you may be able to shorten the total time by engaging in overlapping activities. For example, while your committee is re- viewing your literature review, you might begin writing your questionnaire. If so, prepare a graphic timeline such as the one shown here (in part) in Example 2.

Example 2

Graphic Timeline for Completion of Research (Partial)	Jan.	Feb.
1. Complete literature review	XXXXXXXXXXXX	
2. Have literature review reviewed by chair		XXXXXX
3. Have literature review reviewed by other committee members		XXXXXX
4. Obtain mailing list from University Data Center		XXXXXX
5. Prepare survey cover letter and first draft of questionnaire		XXX

Note: XXX = one week; XXXXXX = two weeks; and so on.

Exercise for Topic 48

1. Prepare a timeline for your proposed research.

Topic 49

Preparing a Reference List

The reference list at the end of a proposal should provide the references for all earlier citations.

The first step in preparing a reference list is to select a *style manual* to guide you in the preparation of the list. The most popular style manual in the social and behavioral sciences is the *Publication Manual of the American Psychological Association* (APA Style Manual), which can be purchased at most college bookstores or online at www.APA.org.

The following list of three references illustrates the APA style specifications for a reference list. Note that the references are in alphabetical order by the first author's surname, which is not necessarily the order in which they were cited earlier in the proposal.

Doe, J. (2010). A hypothetical study on a hypothetical treatment for aggressive behavior. *Journal of Hypothetical Treatments, 33,* 145–192.

Jones, B., & Solis, K. (2009). Correlation between grades and scores on an aggression scale. *Educational Journal of Speculative Studies, 12,* 15–21.

Smith, V. (2010). *Toward a theory of social aggression.* Chicago: Hypothetical Publishing.

The first two references in the above reference list are for *journal articles.* Note the following in these two references:

- The titles of the journals are italicized (or underlined if italics are not available).

- The volume number (e.g., *33* in the first reference) is italicized. For most journals, each year of publication is treated as a separate volume; the first year is Volume 1, the second year is Volume 2, and so on.

- Within each year, each issue of a journal has an issue number. In APA style, issue numbers are *not* included in the references.[1]

- The last two numbers in each reference (e.g., 145–192 in the first reference) are the page numbers encompassing the entire journal article. Note that abbreviations for "page numbers" such as "pp." are *not* used in APA style.

- When there is more than one author, the symbol "&"—*not* the word "and"—is used.

- Pay special attention to the punctuation throughout the reference list. For instance, there is a period after the close of the parentheses around the year of publication.

The last reference in the list above refers to a book. For variations such as subsequent editions of a book and a chapter in an edited book, consult the APA manual.

Great care should be used in the preparation of a reference list. Failure to prepare an accurate and properly format-

---

[1] See the APA Style Manual for rare exceptions.

ted list might call into question a writer's
ability to write an accurate report of the
proposed research.

Exercise for Topic 49

1. Have you selected a style manual to follow when preparing the reference list? If so, name it.

2. Will you be including references to materials not covered in this chapter (e.g., a convention report or a paper published on the Web)? If so, does the style manual you selected cover how to format the references to them? Explain.

Part K

Model Research Proposals for Discussion

In this part of the book, you will find nine model proposals. All are solid proposals. However, expectations for proposals vary according to purpose. For instance, a proposal written as a term project in a research methods class may be acceptable with less detail than one written for dissertation research. Thus, the following proposals are presented to be used as starting points for discussion in class. This will permit instructors to point out which parts of each proposal meet their expectations for the proposals their students will be writing. In addition, after reading the proposals, students may raise questions about how they might serve as models for their own work.

Notes

Model Proposal 1: A Survey

Collegiate Athletic Trainers' Knowledge and Perceptions of Disordered Eating Behaviors in Athletes[1]

A Research Proposal Based on the Work of

Amy Thompson

Debra Boardley

Faith Yingling

Joan Rocks

ABSTRACT

To assess athletic trainers' perceptions and knowledge regarding disordered eating behaviors and to estimate their confidence in response to a test of knowledge, a cross-sectional mail questionnaire will be distributed to a national random sample of 500 athletic trainers from the National Collegiate Athletic Association and National Association of Intercollegiate Athletics. A 30-item questionnaire will assess perceptions of disordered eating behaviors within five domains. Opinions regarding the prevalence of disordered eating, athletic injury, and nutritional status, and their role in recognizing disordered eating will be assessed. Descriptive and inferential statistics will be used to analyze the results.

In the past few decades, awareness of the prevalence of disordered eating among college athletes and its effects on health and performance has increased. Current estimates of the prevalence of eating disorders in college athletes vary substantially and range from 1% to 62%, depending on the sport studied, the definition of disordered eating, and the assessment methods (Byrne & McLean, 2001; Reinking & Alexander, 2005). While disordered eating has been reported for both male and female athletes competing in a variety of sports, those competing in sports that emphasize leanness or appearance appear to show increased risk for development of disordered eating (Smolak, Murnen, & Ruble, 2000; Karlson, Becker, & Merkur, 2001).

Role of Athletic Programs

Collegiate athletic programs have been challenged to identify and manage eating disorders. A study by Turk, Prentice, Chappel, and Shields (1999) investigated collegiate coaches' knowledge of disordered eating within five domains of etiology, identifying signs and symptoms, management and treatment, risk factors, and education and prevention. Also, the study assessed confidence coaches had in their responses to knowledge questions. Researchers found that although coaches may feel confident about educating or preventing eating disorders, they may be giving incorrect information to athletes.

---

[1] This proposal was adapted from a report of completed research by Thompson, A., Yingling, F., Boardley, D., & Rocks, J. (2007). Collegiate athletic trainers' knowledge and perceptions of disordered eating behaviors in athletes. *Psychological Reports, 101,* 1173–1178. Copyright © 2007 by Psychological Reports. Reprinted with permission. Correspondence about the completed research may be addressed to Amy Thompson, Department of Adult Counseling, Health, and Vocational Education, Kent State University, P.O. Box 5190, Kent, OH 44242. Electronic mail may be sent to athomp4@kent.edu. The affiliations of the authors are: Amy Thompson, Kent State University; Faith Yingling, Toledo Children's Hospital; Debra Boardley, The University of Toledo; and Joan Rocks, Otterbein College.

A more recent study by Sherman, DeHass, Thompson, and Wilfert (2005) reported that most of the 2,894 coaches they surveyed rated symptoms of eating disorders as serious in terms of athletes' health and performance. These authors observed that athletic trainers are also frequently involved in identification of eating disorders as athletic trainers work closely with both coaches and athletes. As certified members of a health care team, they are involved in the medical supervision of athletes and are often the first to recognize signs of disordered eating.

Research on athletic trainers and disordered eating is limited. One study investigated confidence of athletic trainers in helping athletes with disordered eating (Vaughn, King, & Cottrell, 2004). Although virtually all athletic trainers reported working with at least one female athlete with an eating disorder, only one in four felt confident identifying such a female athlete.

Purpose

The proposed investigation will assess athletic trainers' perception and knowledge of eating disorders to compare results with those of the prior survey of collegiate coaches conducted by Turk et al. (1999). Data from athletic trainers may augment the findings from coaches and could be helpful in prevention and management of disordered eating by college athletes.

Method

Participants

A computerized random sample of 500 athletic trainers from the National Collegiate Athletic Association Divisions I, II, and III, and the National Association of Intercollegiate Athletics colleges across the United States will be mailed questionnaires. Names and addresses of athletic trainers will be randomly chosen from the Blue Book of College Athletics for Senior, Junior, and Community Colleges (Beagley, 2000) using a random-number procedure.

Several techniques will be used to increase the response rate: a $1 incentive; a postage-paid, self-addressed, return envelope; a hand-signed cover letter assuring confidentiality; and use of colored paper (King, Pealer, & Bernard, 2000). Coding will be used to track returns and facilitate follow-up. Approximately two weeks after the initial mailing, a second mailing will be sent to nonrespondents with a second cover letter, another copy of the questionnaire, and a postage-paid return envelope.

Prior to the mailing of the questionnaire, approval will be sought from the university's human subjects committee.

Instrumentation

The survey conducted by Turk et al. (1999) measured coaches' knowledge about disordered eating by their athletes. The questionnaire used in the study by Turk et al. will be adapted slightly to measure such knowledge among athletic trainers. Specifically, the 30 knowledge and confidence items will be modified by substitution of the words "athletic trainer" for "coach."

Turk et al. reported the questionnaire had been reviewed for content validity by 11 experts in athletic training, exercise physiology, nutrition, psychiatry, sports administration, sports psychology, sports science, and sports medicine. Also, 10 coaches examined the items.

After a comprehensive review of eating disorder literature, additional questions may be added to assess opinions regarding disordered eating and the role of athletic trainers in dealing with disordered eating in athletes. Also, questions will be added to gather demographic information about access to programming and educational materials for prevention of disordered eating.

The modified questionnaire will be sent to experts in nutrition, athletic training, exercise science, and psychology for critical comments and feedback on the content validity of the items. The feedback may lead to refinements in the wording of some items.

This process will yield a questionnaire consisting of approximately 50 items on knowledge, confidence in the correctness of each answer, attitudes of the trainers, and demographic data. As in the Turk et al. survey (1999), knowledge will be divided into five sections about specific aspects of disordered eating. Each section will contain six true-false statements about knowledge in the following areas: etiology, identification of potential risk factors, prevention and education, and management and treatment of disordered eating. In addition, athletic trainers will be asked to rate their confidence in their response to each true-false statement on a 4-item Likert scale on which verbal labels will be 1: Not at all confident and 4: Very confident.

The second section of the questionnaire will focus on attitudes toward statements regarding the prevalence of disordered eating among athletes, the role of nutrition in athletic injury, and the athletic trainer's role in the recognition and prevention of disordered eating among athletes. Verbal labels for responses will range from 1: Strongly disagree to 5: Strongly agree.

To estimate stability/reliability, the questionnaire will be distributed twice to a convenience sample of 20 student athletic trainers. The value of the test-retest reliability coefficient will be calculated.

Analysis

First, the response rate (i.e., the percentage of completed questionnaires) will be calculated for the total sample as well as separately for men and women.

Second, the number of correct responses and the percentage correct for each participant in each of the five knowledge domains will be determined. For instance, if a participant marks 5 of the 6 Risk Factors knowledge items correctly, he or she will have a percentage correct of 83.3%. The mean percentage correct for all participants in each domain will then be calculated and reported in a table such as Table 1 below. Likewise, the average percentages of incorrect answers will be calculated and reported.

Third, for each knowledge item, each participant will indicate his or her confidence in the answer on a scale from 1: Not at all confident to 4: Very confident. The mean confidence ratings will be calculated separately for correct and incorrect answers and will also be reported in the table. These means will provide valuable information for use in interpretation of the results. For instance, a high mean percentage correct in a knowledge domain accompanied by a high mean confidence rating would have a very different interpretation from a high mean percentage correct in the knowledge domain accompanied by a low mean confidence rating.

Table 1
Athletic Trainers' Knowledge and Confidence Score* by Domain

Domain	M % Correct	$M_{confidence}$	M % Incorrect	$M_{confidence}$
Risk factors				
Etiology				
Identifying signs and symptoms				
Management and treatment				
Education and prevention				

*Confidence scores report how confident respondents were with the answers to knowledge questions. Each knowledge question will be followed by a confidence ranking using verbal labels for ratings of 1: Not at all confident and 4: Very confident.

Fourth, the results on the knowledge questions in this study with athletic trainers will be compared with the results of Turk et al.'s earlier study of college coaches. This will be done by comparing the percentage of participants in each study who scored between 90% and 100% correct on all knowledge items.

Fifth, the following analyses will be conducted to provide additional insights. In each case, the difference between the total mean knowledge scores for the two groups will be tested with t tests with p equal to or less than .05:

1. Mean knowledge scores of men versus women

2. Mean knowledge scores of participants who attended an educational program within the past year versus those who had not done so

3. Mean knowledge scores of participants who had three or more educational resources on disordered eating (e.g., videos) versus those who did not

Discussion

This study will provide valuable information on the educational needs of athletic trainers at the college level. Because knowledge in five different knowledge domains will be measured separately, the information will be diagnostic (e.g., more emphasis in one knowledge domain might be needed than in another domain in future educational programs for athletic trainers).

Limitations

Three limitations are worthy of note. First, this study will be limited to certified athletic trainers, so it will not be appropriate to generalize the results to trainers who are not certified.

Second, as with almost all mailed questionnaires in the social sciences, a response rate of less than 100% is anticipated. However, due to the $1 incentive and the follow-up mailing, a high rate of return is anticipated. Nevertheless, great caution should be exercised when attempting to generalize to nonrespondents.

Finally, the closed format of the questionnaire will not provide room for participants to express themselves in their own words or to comment on their educational needs on disordered eating. This limitation might be addressed in future studies.

References

Beagley, C. (Ed.). (2000). *The 2000–2001 blue book of college athletics for senior, junior, and community colleges.* Montgomery, AL: Dees Communications.

Byrne, S., & McLean, N. (2001). Eating disorder in athletes: A review of the literature. *Journal of Science and Medicine in Sport, 4,* 145–159.

Karlson, K. A., Becker, C. B., & Merkur, A. (2001). Prevalence of eating disordered behavior in collegiate lightweight women rowers and distance runners. *Clinical Journal of Sport Medicine, 11,* 32–37.

King, K., Pealer, L., & Bernard, A. (2000). Increasing response rate to mail questionnaires: A review of inducement strategies. *American Journal of Health Education, 32,* 4–15.

Reinking, M. F., & Alexander, L. E. (2005). Prevalence of disordered eating behaviors in undergraduate female collegiate athletes and nonathletes. *Journal of Athletic Training, 40,* 47–51.

Sherman, R. T., DeHass, D., Thompson, R. A., & Wilfert, M. (2005). NCAA coaches survey: The role of the coach in identifying and managing athletes with disordered eating. *Eating Disorders: The Journal of Treatment and Prevention, 13,* 447–466.

Smolak, L., Murnen, S. K., & Ruble, A. E. (2000). Female athletes and eating problems: A meta-analysis. *International Journal of Eating Disorders, 27,* 371–380.

Turk, J. C., Prentice, W. E., Chappel, S., & Shields, E. W. (1999). Collegiate coaches' knowledge of eating disorders. *Journal of Athletic Training, 34,* 19–24.

Vaughn, J. L., King, K. A., & Cottrell, R. R. (2004). Collegiate athletic trainers' confidence in helping females with eating disorders. *Journal of Athletic Training, 39,* 71–76.

Model Proposal 2: A Survey

Do Psychologists Adhere to the Clinical Practice Guidelines for Tobacco Cessation? A Survey of Practitioners[1]

A Research Proposal Based on the Work of

Kristin M. Phillips   Thomas H. Brandon

ABSTRACT

Practicing psychologists are well positioned to provide at least minimal interventions for tobacco dependence among their clients. Because smoking covaries with psychopathology, a substantial proportion of psychologists' clients are likely to be smokers. Psychologists have expertise in motivating behavior change, and they have greater contact and stronger relationships with their patients than do most other health providers. The primary purpose of the proposed study is to survey a sample of practicing psychologists to estimate the extent to which they intervene with patients who smoke. Another goal of the study is to determine how often psychologists intervene for tobacco use compared with the frequency with which they intervene for their patients' other risky behaviors, such as alcohol and illicit drug use. In addition, data will be collected on the types of training psychologists have had for intervening for tobacco use and reasons why they do not intervene for such use.

How can psychologists reduce the public health burden of tobacco use? Tobacco smoking is the single greatest preventable cause of premature mortality and morbidity in the United States. Nevertheless, approximately one in four adults in the United States continues to smoke (Centers for Disease Control and Prevention [CDC], 2002). Few interventions provided by psychologists have greater potential to save clients' lives than assistance with smoking cessation.

The basic steps that primary care clinicians (including psychologists) should take to intervene with their smoking patients have been formalized into the U.S. Public Health Service's clinical practice guidelines, originally published in 1996 and updated in 2000 (Fiore et al., 2000). The meta-analyses reported in these guidelines provided evidence that (a) both assessing for tobacco use and advising patients to quit smoking increased cessation rates, and (b) the more intensive the intervention, the greater the cessation rates. For example, compared with no contact, the estimated abstinence rates associated with minimal counseling (less than 3 min), low-intensity counseling (3–10 min), and higher-intensity counseling (more than 10 min) were 13.4%, 16.0%, and 22.1% respectively, compared with 10.9% with no contact. Consequently, the guidelines recommend that clinicians assess for tobacco use among all patients and that they intervene regardless of whether tobacco use was the reason for the patient's visit.

---

[1] This proposal was adapted from a report of completed research by Phillips, K. M., & Brandon, T. H. (2004). Do psychologists adhere to the clinical practice guidelines for tobacco cessation? A survey of practitioners. *Professional Psychology: Research and Practice*, *35*, 281–285. Copyright © 2004 by the American Psychological Association, Inc. Reprinted with permission. Correspondence about the completed research may be addressed to Thomas H. Brandon, Department of Psychology, University of South Florida, PCD 4118G, 4202 East Fowler Avenue, Tampa, FL 33620-7200. Electronic mail may be sent to brandont@moffitt.usf.edu. The affiliations of the authors are: Kristin M. Phillips, Department of Psychology, University of Miami; and Thomas H. Brandon, Department of Psychology, University of South Florida.

The guidelines recommend 5 steps, the 5 "A"s, of a minimal intervention in clinical settings: (a) *ask* whether patients use tobacco, (b) *advise* patients to quit, (c) *assess* patients' willingness to quit, (d) *assist* those patients who are willing to quit, and (e) *arrange* follow-up contact to avoid relapse. Implementing these steps requires, at minimum, approximately 3 minutes of a clinician's time.

To elaborate, all clinicians should have a systematic routine for identifying smokers at every visit. After *asking* a patient about smoking and providing strong, clear, and personalized *advice* to quit, clinicians should also *assess* patients' willingness to quit. Clinicians can *assist* willing patients by providing support or educational material, identifying personal barriers, referring to a cessation clinic or behavior specialist, providing pharmacological or behavioral treatment, setting a quit date, or negotiating an intervention plan. After a patient's visit, it is important to *arrange* follow-up with the patient to assess progress and help to prevent relapse. Follow-up can take place at the next office visit or by phone, mail, or—with appropriate precautions—e-mail (Fiore et al., 2000).

Dissemination of the guidelines has focused on physicians as the clinicians with the greatest opportunities to intervene with smoking patients. However, considerable research indicates that physicians do not reliably do so. That is, although surveys of physicians themselves generally find that more than 50% of physicians claim to regularly counsel smokers to quit (e.g., Fortmann, Sallis, Magnus, & Farquhar, 1985; Wells, Lewis, Leake, Schleiter, & Brook, 1986), surveys of patients indicate that fewer than 50% have received advice to quit from their physicians (e.g., CDC, 1993; Doescher & Saver, 2000; Gilpin et al., 1992). Direct observation of physicians' behavior has yielded similar findings (Ellerbeck, Ahluwalia, Jolicoeur, Gladden, & Mosier, 2001).

Although physicians may have the greatest credibility when giving health-related advice, psychologists have other advantages (Groth-Marnat & Schumaker, 1995; Wetter et al., 1998). First, cigarette smoking is associated with psychological disorders, such as major depression, anxiety disorders, schizophrenia, and alcohol dependence. Thus, a substantial proportion of practicing psychologists' clientele may use tobacco and be at particular risk for tobacco-related illnesses. Lasser et al. (2000) concluded that persons with a diagnosable mental disorder consumed nearly half of all cigarettes in the United States. Second, psychologists have training and expertise in motivating behavior change. Both specific and nonspecific therapeutic skills may be put to use by psychologists to motivate and facilitate smoking cessation among their patients. A third advantage of psychologists over physicians is that, in many cases, there is a stronger, more enduring relationship between psychologists and their patients. The frequent, regular, and relatively lengthy sessions of typical psychotherapy provide an opportunity for more systematic, intensive, and consistent intervention compared with the typically short, rushed, and infrequent physician-patient encounters. Moreover, the nature of the therapeutic relationship between psychologist and patient may compensate for the lessened medical credibility of the psychologist as compared with the physician.

In contrast to studies of physician behavior, to date no published reports have described the degree to which practicing psychologists intervene with patients who smoke. This is the primary aim of the present study. To add context to psychologists' self-reported intervention efforts for tobacco use, we will also assess their reported efforts for other risky client behaviors. This has the additional benefit of obscuring from participants the true focus of the survey. We hypothesize that psychologists are less likely to intervene for tobacco use than for illicit drug abuse and alcohol abuse, more traditional targets of assessment and treatment.

Survey of Smoking Cessation Interventions

An original two-page survey will be developed to assess clinicians' efforts with regard to six patterns of potentially risky behavior among clients: tobacco use, alcohol abuse, illicit drug abuse, problem gambling, reckless driving, and unsafe sex. Alcohol and drug abuse will be included to provide a comparison with behaviors that traditionally receive more clinical attention than tobacco use. Reckless driving will be included as a validity check, as this is a behavior that is not expected to receive much clinical attention. We have no strong expectancies about how gambling and unsafe sex will compare with tobacco use in eliciting clinician action because these behaviors share with tobacco use a relatively short history of clinical attention. The addition of the five comparison risky behaviors also will serve to obscure the true focus of the survey on tobacco-related actions.

The first six questions will address participants' use of the 5 "A"s (ask, advise, assess, assist, and arrange follow-up) for each of the six risky behaviors. The assist action will require two questions: one about making referrals to specialists and one about providing treatment oneself. The answer format for these first six questions will be a 7-point Likert-type scale (1 = *with no patients*, 2 = *with some patients*, 3 = *with a little less than half of patients*, 4 = *with half of patients*, 5 = *with a little more than half of patients*, 6 = *with most patients*, and 7 = *with all patients*). The questions will be written so that later questions are independent of answers to earlier ones. For example, the advising and assessing questions will be based on the premise that the clinician had somehow learned about the risky behavior, regardless of whether they reported asking patients about the behavior. Similarly, the assist and arrange questions will presume that the clinician learned that the patient was willing to change. In remaining questions, participants will be asked to indicate the types of training they received for intervening with each of the six behaviors and the barriers to intervening.

The Sample

Surveys will be sent to 1,000 psychologists randomly selected from the membership of the American Psychological Association (APA), with the following inclusion criteria: They are residents of the United States, hold doctoral degrees, and have paid a supplemental practitioner assessment. The list will be rented from APA, which will conduct the random selection and provide mailing labels to the investigators.

As with all mail surveys, it is anticipated that a large percentage of those who are contacted by mail will not respond. However, with an initial list of 1,000 psychologists, it is reasonable to assume that at least 250 will respond. We expect that the overall response rate will be reduced because some of the 1,000 targeted psychologists will have retired or died and others will not work with adult or adolescent patients.

The survey will collect demographic data on the respondents, including race/ethnicity, gender, highest degree earned (i.e., Ph.D., Psy.D., or Ed.D.), and years of clinical practice. These data will allow a comparison of the respondents with the description provided by APA of the full target sample of 1,000 psychologists. This will indicate the extent to which the final sample of respondents is representative of the target sample.

Analysis

Likelihood of Intervention for Tobacco Use

The primary purpose of the proposed study is to describe the degree to which practicing psychologists intervene with patients who smoke. For this purpose, the percentage of psychologists who report engaging in each of the "A"s (i.e., ask, advise, assess, assist by referring, assist by providing treatment, and arranging follow-up) will be computed.

Comparison with Other Risky Behaviors

Another goal of the study is to determine how often psychologists intervene for tobacco use compared with the frequency with which they intervene for their patients' other risky behaviors. For this purpose, means will be computed for each of the Likert-type items. For instance, the mean score (on a scale from 1 to 7) for "Ask" for tobacco will be computed. Likewise, the mean score for "Ask" for alcohol will be computed. In all, there will be 36 means that will be presented in a table such as Table 1.

Table 1
Use of the 5 "A"s

Clinician action (5 "A"s)	Means[a]					
	Tobacco	Alcohol	Illicit drugs	Unsafe sex	Reckless driving	Gambling
Ask						
Advise						
Assess						
Assist						
Arrange						

[a]Means will be based on a Likert-type scale ranging from 1 (*with no patients*) to 7 (*with all patients*).

For each intervention, a within-group analysis of variance (ANOVA) will be conducted to compare responses to the types of risky behaviors, with significance being determined at the $p < .001$ level. Simple comparisons will then be conducted for each intervention, comparing the likelihood ratings for tobacco use with each of the other risky behaviors. Specifically, this part of the analysis will determine whether there are significant differences between the following:
1. Intervention for tobacco use versus alcohol
2. Intervention for tobacco use versus illicit drugs
3. Intervention for tobacco use versus unsafe sex
4. Intervention for tobacco use versus reckless driving
5. Intervention for tobacco use versus gambling

Training and Education

Percentages of respondents who report each of the following types of training for intervention for tobacco use will be reported:
1. Read about topic
2. Attended single workshop
3. Attended multiple workshops
4. Clinical coursework
5. Has this as an area of expertise
6. Has this as the primary area of expertise
7. Has some other type of training
8. Has no training or expertise

Barriers to Intervention

Percentages of respondents who report each of the following reasons for not intervening for tobacco use will be reported:
1. Not patient's presenting problem
2. Concern that patient may not be receptive
3. Lack of relevant training
4. Lack of relevant skills
5. May interfere with other therapy goals
6. Not seen by clinician as a risk for patient
7. Other reason
8. Lack of time
9. Not reimbursed for this type of counseling

Discussion

The primary aim of this study is to assess the degree to which practicing psychologists attend to their clients' tobacco use.

The degree to which psychologists are ignoring tobacco use among their clients will be brought into focus through comparisons with their actions regarding clients' alcohol abuse or illicit drug use. For reasons described elsewhere (Miller & Brown, 1997), psychologists have traditionally shied away from treating such substance abuse. We anticipate that the respondents will report being more likely to ask, advise, and assess for alcohol abuse and illicit drug use than for tobacco use. This is predicted because there is a history of greater societal concern about these behaviors than about tobacco use. Although the potential adverse social and medical consequences of alcohol and illicit drug abuse tend to be more immediate than the consequences of tobacco use, the delayed effects of tobacco use are substantial. Not only does tobacco use account for far greater mortality than alcohol and illicit drug use combined, but the probability of a given smoker dying prematurely from a smoking-related illness approaches 50%.

There are two notable limitations to the data that will be collected. First, they will be derived from self-reported clinician behavior rather than from client reports or direct observation. Among physicians, self-reports of intervening for tobacco use tend to be higher than reports of their patients or reports of observers. We would expect a similar pattern to emerge among psychologists, suggesting that the reported intervention rates are likely to be somewhat inflated. The second limitation is that a low response rate is expected. Unfortunately, low rates are not atypical among surveys of practitioners. In addition, it is likely that individuals with interests in substance abuse and those who could endorse the intervention behaviors will be the most likely to complete the questionnaire. Thus, although these two limitations may distort the intervention rates reported, they most likely will do so by inflating the reported rates. Therefore, it is reasonable to consider the rates that will be reported in this research to be the probable upper limits of the true rates at which psychologists intervene with tobacco use and other risky client behaviors.

References

Centers for Disease Control and Prevention. (1993). Physician and other health-care professional counseling of smokers to quit: United States, 1991. *Morbidity and Mortality Weekly Report, 42*, 854–857.

Centers for Disease Control and Prevention. (2002). Cigarette smoking among adults—United States, 2000. *Morbidity and Mortality Weekly Report, 51*, 642–645.

Doescher, M. P., & Saver, B. G. (2000). Physician's advice to quit smoking: The glass remains half empty. *Journal of Family Practice, 48*, 543–553.

Ellerbeck, E. F., Ahluwalia, J. S., Jolicoeur, D. G., Gladden, J., & Mosier, M. C. (2001). Direct observation of smoking cessation activities in primary care practice. *Journal of Family Practice, 50*, 688–693.

Fiore, M. C., Bailey, W. C., & Cohen, S. J. (2000). Treating tobacco use and dependence. (et al. Clinical Practice Guideline. Rockville, MD: U.S. Department of Health and Human Services, Public Health Service.)

Fortmann, S. P., Sallis, J. F., Magnus, P. M., & Farquhar, J. W. (1985). Attitudes and practices of physicians regarding hypertension and smoking: The Stanford Five City Project. *Preventive Medicine, 14*, 70–80.

Gilpin, E., Pierce, J., Goodman, J., Giovino, G., Berry, C., & Burns, D. (1992). Trends in physicians' giving advice to stop smoking: United States, 1974–1987. *Tobacco Control, 1*, 31–36.

Groth-Marnat, G., & Schumaker, J. (1995). Psychologists in disease prevention and health promotion: A review of the cost-effectiveness literature. *Psychology: A Journal of Human Behavior, 32*, 1–10.

Lasser, K., Boyd, J. W., Woolhandler, S., Himmelstein, D. U., McCormick, D., & Bor, D. H. (2000). Smoking and mental illness: A population-based prevalence study. *Journal of the American Medical Association, 284*, 2606–2610.

Miller, W. R., & Brown, S. A. (1997). Why psychologists should treat alcohol and drug problems. *American Psychologist, 52*, 1269–1279.

Wells, K. B., Lewis, C. E., Leake, B., Schleiter, M. K., & Brook, R. H. (1986). The practices of general and subspecialty internists in counseling about smoking and exercise. *American Journal of Public Health, 76*, 1009–1013.

Wetter, D. W., Fiore, M. C., Gritz, E. R., Lando, H. A., Stitzer, M. L., Hasselblad, V., & Baker, T. B. (1998). The Agency for Health Care Policy and Research Smoking Cessation Clinical Practice Guideline: Findings and implications for psychologists. *American Psychologist, 53*, 657–669.

Notes

Model Proposal 3: Test Development Research

The Americans With Disabilities Act Knowledge Survey[1]

A Research Proposal Based on the Work of

Brigida Hernandez   Christopher Keys

Fabricio Balcazar

ABSTRACT

Objectives: To construct and validate a measure that assesses knowledge of the Americans With Disabilities Act (ADA). *Study design and subjects*: The new 20-item measure will be administered to approximately 200 undergraduates and 30 ADA experts to establish validity and reliability. *Anticipated results*: The ADA experts will obtain a significantly higher mean score than the undergraduates, which will provide an indication of the measure's validity. Reliability analysis will be conducted by computing Cronbach's alpha, with an alpha of .80 or more expected.

Census figures indicate that approximately 53 million noninstitutionalized Americans have physical, sensory, intellectual, or psychiatric disabilities. Of these, 33 million individuals have disabilities that are classified as severe (McNeil, 2001). Passed in 1990, the Americans With Disabilities Act (ADA) is intended to fully include people with disabilities in all aspects of mainstream U.S. culture. To date, it is the most comprehensive law concerning disability rights. Consisting of five titles, the ADA encompasses areas of employment, public services, transportation, public accommodations, and telecommunications. Many individuals are required to comply with this law, including employers, business owners, and providers of goods and services. Success of the ADA is heavily dependent on their actions and knowledge of this law.

A review of the literature indicates that 12 studies have examined ADA knowledge among various groups, including managers, personnel directors, human resource representatives, employers, occupational therapists, adults with disabilities, and students of rehabilitation counseling (see Table 1). Nine studies used self-report items (e.g., "Have you ever heard of the ADA?" and "How knowledgeable are you about the ADA?") to assess knowledge of this law (Bruch, 1998; Ehrhart, 1995; Kregel & Tomiyasu, 1994; Louis Harris and Associates, 1994, 1998; Roessler & Sumner, 1997; Scheid, 1999; Walters & Baker, 1996; Waters & Johanson, 2001), with most respondents indicating some knowledge about the ADA. Only three studies administered an actual test to assess knowledge of the ADA titles (Clarke & Crewe, 2000; Redick, McClain, & Brown, 2000; Thakker & Solomon, 1999). It is interesting to note that these studies suggested a low level of ADA knowledge among employers, college students with disabilities, and occupational thera-

[1] This proposal was adapted from a report of completed research by Hernandez, B., Keys, C., & Balcazar, F. (2003). The Americans With Disabilities Act knowledge survey: Strong psychometrics and weak knowledge. *Rehabilitation Psychology*, 48, 93–99. Copyright © 2003 by The Educational Publishing Foundation. Reprinted with permission. Correspondence about the completed research may be addressed to Christopher Keys, Department of Psychology, DePaul University, 2219 North Kenmore Avenue, Chicago, IL 60614. Electronic mail may be sent to ckeys@depaul.edu. The current affiliations of the authors are: Brigida Hernandez and Christopher Keys, Department of Psychology, DePaul University; and Fabricio Balcazar, Department of Disability and Human Development, University of Illinois at Chicago. The authors appreciate the feedback of Daniel Keys on an earlier draft of this proposal.

pists. However, to date, a psychometrically sound measure of ADA knowledge that is both valid and reliable has not been developed. In addition, demographic and job-related correlates of ADA knowledge have not been fully examined. Thus far, three studies have examined the relationship between company size and ADA knowledge; all three found that respondents from larger companies reported more knowledge than those from smaller companies (Ehrhart, 1995; Scheid, 1999; Waters & Johanson, 2001).

Table 1

Studies That Assessed Knowledge of the Americans With Disabilities Act (ADA)

Study	n and type of participants	Approximate establishment size	Results
Ehrhart (1995)[a]	373 national managers of manufacturing, wholesale trade, retail trade, business/legal/engineering services, education/health/social services, & government	25–1,000+ employees	72% rated themselves as being knowledgeable to very knowledgeable of the ADA as a whole, with those from larger establishments rating themselves as more knowledgeable than those from smaller ones
Roessler & Sumner (1997)[a]	83 national personnel & human resource representatives of manufacturing, financial services, & retail establishments	57% had > 500 employees	75% reported being very familiar with the ADA employment site
Louis Harris and Associates (1994)[a]	1,021 adults with disabilities; national survey		58% had not heard or read ADA-related material
Louis Harris and Associates (1998)[a]	1,000 adults with disabilities; national survey		46% had not heard or read ADA-related material
Thakker & Solomon (1999)	195 supervisors & managers of social service, medical, real estate, manufacturing, & service establishments	15 or more employees	90% reported being somewhat or very familiar with the ADA: a 19-item true-false measure of ADA knowledge was developed & administered; α = .73; mean score of this measure with this sample was not reported
Kregel & Tomiyasu (1994)[a]	170 local employers of retail, manufacturing services, & government businesses	1–249 employees	96% reported being aware that the ADA prohibits employment discrimination
Scheid (1999)[a]	117 local human resource managers & personnel directors of mostly retail, trade, manufacturing, health services, & government establishments	from < 100 to > 1,000 employees	79% received formal information about the ADA, with respondents from larger establishments being more likely to have received such information than those from smaller ones
Clarke & Crewe (2000)	83 small business employers, 62 college students with disabilities, 57 master's-level rehabilitation counseling students	not reported & not applicable for two of three samples	50-item ADA Information Survey was developed & administered to assess knowledge of Title I (employment); α = .53; rehabilitation counseling students attained the highest scores
Walters & Baker (1996)[a]	69 local employers, 19 recruiters (university job fair), & 12 recruiters (disability job fair) of sales, service, manufacturing, food industry, & health care establishments	1–14 full time (41%) & 1–14 part time (56%) employees	88% reported being familiar with the ADA
Waters & Johanson (2001)[a]	87 local employment managers; type of establishment not reported	54% had 15 or more employees	Respondents from larger companies reported greater familiarity with & understanding of the ADA's definition of "disabled" and "reasonable accommodations" than those from smaller ones
Bruch (1998)[a]	55 local human resource specialists & managers of financial, educational, retail, health, manufacturing, service, industrial, social service, & warehouse establishments	93% had > 100 employees	94% reported being at least somewhat knowledgeable of ADA Title I (employment)
Redick, McClain, & Brown (2000)	152 occupational therapists; national survey		10-point ADA Title III (public accommodations) quiz was developed; mean score was 1.85 (SD = 1.64); reliability & validity information not reported

[a]These studies used solely respondents' self-reports to assess ADA knowledge.

The four objectives of this study are to (a) construct and establish the validity and reliability of a measure that assesses knowledge of the ADA, (b) empirically examine knowledge of this law among private- and public-sector representatives, (c) identify demographic and job-related correlates of ADA knowledge, and (d) compare perceived and actual knowledge of the ADA. More specifically, the first study will develop and validate the ADA Knowledge Survey. This new measure taps knowledge concerning the three major ADA titles: Title I prohibits discrimination in the realm of employment, Title II ensures that eligible individuals with disabilities are not denied state and local government services because of their disabilities, and Title III prohibits discrimination against people with disabilities in the full and equal enjoyment of goods, services, and facilities open to the public. To assess validity (criterion groups validity), scores obtained from university students will be compared with those obtained from individuals with ADA expertise. The reliability assessment will consist of calculating Cronbach's alpha, a measure of internal consistency, using the entire sample of university students and ADA experts.

Study 1: Construction and Validation of the ADA Knowledge Survey

Method

Sample

Participants will consist of two groups. The first will be approximately 200 students enrolled in introductory psychology courses at an urban Midwestern university. It is anticipated that almost all will be 20 years old or younger. The second group will consist of at least 30 ADA experts. It is anticipated that the vast majority of the experts will be 30 years old or older and hold graduate degrees. These individuals direct, manage, and/or work for projects and organizations that promote training and awareness of disability issues to the public.

Instrument

The ADA Knowledge Survey will consist of approximately 20 items that will be created following a review of the ADA titles and Whittle's (1993) *Americans With Disabilities Act of 1990 True or False Quiz.* Items will target Title I (employment), Title II (state and local government services), and Title III (public accommodations). Items will address these three titles because they are the ones primarily implemented by representatives of the private and public sector. Additional items will be general items that relate to all titles.

For each item, a true-false format that includes a "do not know" option will be used. The sum of correct responses will represent an overall ADA knowledge score. A team of disability professionals with in-depth knowledge of the ADA will review these items for accuracy, clarity, completeness, and legal sufficiency. Following reviews by this team, items will be modified and the final version of the survey will be finalized. Reviewers will include the director of an ADA Disability and Business Technical Assistance Center, a staff representative of the National Institute on Disability and Rehabilitation Research, an attorney with ADA expertise, and two active researchers in the field of disabilities and disability rights.

Procedures

The university students will complete the ADA Knowledge Survey in supervised group settings of approximately 25 participants each. They will receive course credit for their participation. The ADA experts will complete the knowledge survey individually.

Analysis and Anticipated Results

A table of results that displays the ADA Knowledge Survey items will be prepared, the title targeted by each item, and the percentage of correct responses per item obtained by each of the two groups. The ranges of scores obtained on the ADA Knowledge Survey for each group will also be reported. Mean scores for university students and for ADA experts will be computed. A t test using the $p < .01$ level will be conducted to determine the significance of the difference between the means for the two groups. If the instrument is valid, the students' mean score should be significantly lower than the experts' mean score. Reliability analysis of the ADA Knowledge Survey, with the entire sample of university students and ADA experts, will be conducted by computing Cronbach's alpha, with the expectation that it will be .80 or higher.

Thus, in this study, an instrument that measures knowledge of the ADA will be constructed and data will be collected to determine if it is psychometrically sound. Face validity will be established with reviews by a team of disability professionals with an in-depth knowledge of the ADA. This team will also review the item content to assure that each targeted its intended title. To demonstrate the criterion group validity of this measure, university students are expected to obtain a significantly lower mean than ADA experts. Reliability assessment is expected to indicate that the ADA Knowledge Survey has good internal consistency.

General Discussion

As the passage of the ADA occurred over a decade ago, it becomes increasingly important to step back and assess knowledge of this groundbreaking civil rights law. In particular, close attention needs to be paid to individuals who are critical agents of change (including employers, managers, personnel directors, and human resource representatives). Past research suggests adequate ADA knowledge among such individuals. However, these studies have relied primarily on self-report assessments. Thus, a main purpose of this study will be to develop a valid and reliable measure that assesses knowledge by asking specific questions about the ADA titles.

Future research should examine knowledge of the ADA with psychometrically sound measures. Insofar as we can determine, if the results are as anticipated, the ADA Knowledge Survey will represent the first psychometrically sound measure to assess this domain. Disability researchers, rehabilitation psychologists, and others can use this new measure to (a) evaluate the needs of particular segments of the population who are critical to successful ADA implementation, such as people with disabilities, business owners, service providers, and employers; (b) evaluate the effectiveness of ADA training and educational efforts; and (c) examine the relationship between ADA knowledge and attitudes toward disability rights and other relevant variables (Hernandez, Keys, Balcazar, & Drum, 1998).

Given the importance of the ADA in the lives of people with disabilities, it behooves rehabilitation professionals, employees of centers for independent living, and others working in the field of disabilities to become more aware of both measures and levels of ADA knowledge among their clients. The ADA Knowledge Survey provides a means to assess and then strengthen knowledge of this law. With increased knowledge of disability rights legislation, people with disabilities are in a better position to advocate for their civil rights as they aim to be fully included in all aspects of mainstream U.S. culture.

A limitation of this study involves its breadth of participant groups. The measure will be validated using college students and disability experts. However, two other groups for which it is intended will not be included: business people and facility managers who implement the ADA and people with disabilities themselves whose civil rights the law is intended to secure and who bear much of the responsibility for enforcing its provisions in practice. Further research will be needed to determine the usefulness of this measure for assessing the ADA knowledge of people with disabilities and business owners and facility managers who are responsible for the accessibility of their public accommodations.

In conclusion, the ADA Knowledge Survey will represent a first step to gaining more accurate assessments of ADA knowledge. With the development of this valid and reliable measure, researchers and disability advocates may assess knowledge of this law among stakeholders with greater accuracy than self-reporting affords. Such assessments are deemed appropriate, given that the ADA is in its second decade and there are indications that knowledge of this law is quite limited, even among those who are most responsible for its implementation.

References

Americans With Disabilities Act of 1990. (1990). (Pub. L. No. 101-336, 42 U.S.C. § 12101).

Bruch, L. A. (1998). Implementation of the Americans With Disabilities Act: Employer commitment to Title I and implications for hiring in northeastern Pennsylvania. *Dissertation Abstracts International, 58*, 4498. Doctoral dissertation, George Washington University, 1997.

Clarke, N. E., & Crewe, N. M. (2000). Stakeholder attitudes toward ADA Title I: Development of an indirect measurement method. *Rehabilitation Counseling Bulletin, 43*, 58–65.

Ehrhart, L. M. (1995). A national study of employers' attitudes toward persons with disabilities. *Dissertation Abstracts International, 55*, 1802. Doctoral dissertation, Virginia Commonwealth University, 1994.

Hernandez, B., Keys, C., Balcazar, F., & Drum, C. (1998). Construction and validation of the Disability Rights Attitude Scale: Assessing attitudes toward the Americans With Disabilities Act (ADA). *Rehabilitation Psychology, 43*, 203–218.

Kregel, J., & Tomiyasu, Y. (1994). Employers' attitudes toward workers with disabilities: Effect of the Americans With Disabilities Act. *Journal of Vocational Rehabilitation, 4*, 165–173.

Louis Harris and Associates. (1994). *The National Organization on Disability/Louis Harris and Associates survey of Americans with disabilities.* New York: Author.

Louis Harris and Associates. (1998). *The National Organization on Disability/Louis Harris and Associates survey of Americans with disabilities.* New York: Author.

McNeil, J. (2001). *Americans with disabilities: 1997 (Series P70–73).* Washington, DC: U.S. Census Bureau.

Redick, A. G., McClain, L., & Brown, C. (2000). Consumer empowerment through occupational therapy: The Americans With Disabilities Act Title III. *American Journal of Occupational Therapy, 54*, 207–213.

Roessler, R. T., & Sumner, G. (1997). Employer opinions about accommodating employees with chronic illness. *Journal of Applied Rehabilitation Counseling, 28*, 29–34.

Scheid, T. L. (1999). Employment of individuals with mental disabilities: Business response to the ADA's challenge. *Behavioral Sciences and the Law, 17*, 73–91.

Thakker, D., & Solomon, P. (1999). Factors influencing managers' adherence to the Americans With Disabilities Act. *Administration and Policy in Mental Health, 26*, 213–219.

U.S. Bureau of the Census. (1996a). *Hispanic-owned businesses: Reaching new heights* (Statistical Brief No. SB/96-4). Washington, DC: U.S. Department of Commerce.

U.S. Bureau of the Census. (1996b). *Warmer, older, more diverse: State-by-state population changes to 2025* (Census Brief No. CENBR/96-1). Washington, DC: U.S. Department of Commerce.

Walters, S. E., & Baker, C. M. (1996). Title I of the Americans With Disabilities Act: Employer and recruiter attitudes toward individuals with disabilities. *Journal of Rehabilitation Administration, 20*, 15–23.

Waters, K. M., & Johanson, J. C. (2001). Awareness and perceived impact of the Americans With Disabilities Act among human resources professionals in three Minnesota cities. *Journal of Disability Policy Studies, 12*, 47–54.

Whittle, W. (1993). *Americans With Disabilities Act of 1990 True or False Quiz.* Unpublished measure.

Notes

Notes

Model Proposal 4: Single-Subject Research

The Effect of a Self-Monitored Relaxation Breathing Exercise on Male Adolescent Aggressive Behavior[1]

A Research Proposal Based on the Work of

Trudi Gaines   Leasha M. Barry

ABSTRACT

This study will contribute to the identification of effective interventions in the area of male adolescent aggressive behavior. Existing research includes both group- and single-case studies implementing treatments that typically include an anger-management component and its attendant relaxation and stress-reduction techniques. The design of this study is single-subject with multiple baselines across six subjects on two behavioral measures. The setting will be a residential juvenile justice program for male adolescents, and the treatment will be a relaxation breathing exercise. The results of the study will be expressed as improvement on both behavioral measures in each of the six participants.

Aggression is a focus of therapeutic interventions with adolescents already involved in the legal system and who may well be on their way to establishing intractable behavior patterns. These patterns may be carried into adulthood and will likely result in criminal activity and incarceration with recidivism reported as high as 50% (Snyder & Sickmund, 1999). While not all adolescents with aggression problems will follow this developmental path, almost all incarcerated adults bring a history of delinquency and aggression with them into their troubled existence (Kazdin, Siegel, & Bass, 1992). The World Health Organization has reported violence as being a global health problem, and so, to intervene effectively in an early stage of this problem's development holds important social merit (Krug, Dahlberg, Mercy, Zwi, & Lozano, 2002).

According to Goldstein, Glick, and Gibbs (1998), the definition of aggression derives from social learning theory and therefore constitutes learned behavior that stems from the interaction of the individual with the environment. The development of violent conduct as reported by Nietzel, Hasemann, and Lynam (1999) occurs when biological, environmental, psychological, and social factors blend in certain patterns. These definitions and origins notwithstanding, the point at which the individual responds to the stimulus, in either a deliberate or an automatic fashion, contains elements that can be ameliorated regardless of the aforementioned factors and origins.

Researchers have focused on aggressive behavior among adolescents in various environments including education (Frey, Hirschstein, & Guzzo, 2000; Deffenbacher, Lynch, Oetting, & Kemper, 1996), corrections (Steiner, Garcia, & Matthews, 1997; Swenson & Kennedy, 1995), and mental health treatment settings (Margolin, Youga, & Ballou, 2002; Snyder, 1999). The au-

---

[1] This proposal was adapted from a report of completed research by Gaines, T., & Barry, L. M. (2008). The effect of a self-monitored relaxation breathing exercise on male adolescent aggressive behavior. *Adolescence, 43,* 291–302. Copyright © 2008 by Libra Publishers, Inc. Reprinted with permission. Correspondence about the completed research may be addressed to Trudi Gaines, Division of Teacher Education, University of West Florida, Building 85, Room 176, 11000 University Parkway, Pensacola, FL, 32514. Electronic mail may be sent to tgaines@uwf.edu. The affiliations of the authors are: Trudi Gaines, Division of Teacher Education, University of West Florida; and Leasha M. Barry, Division of Teacher Education, University of West Florida.

thors of this proposed study seek to contribute to efforts that identify effective prevention measures that educators and other professionals who work with adolescents can incorporate into a variety of settings that are cost effective and entail the least disruption to normal daily activities and routines.

Anger Management Interventions

Anger management interventions typically include relaxation exercises for stress and anxiety reduction, and these exercises often focus on deep breathing (Fraser, 1996). When adolescents learned about the physiology of anger and how to use the techniques that promote relaxation and self-regulation, teachers, parents, and the adolescents themselves reported improvement in their behavior (Kellner, 1999). The recommendations made by Rutherford, Quinn, and Mathur (1996) described an approach to aggression and problem behaviors that included the various components of social skills training, cooperative learning, anger management, and self-control strategies. The anger management component emphasized the teaching of specific relaxation and stress-reduction breathing exercises, which included deep breathing and deep muscle relaxation. Other relaxation techniques that have been shown to be useful in arousal reduction are progressive muscle relaxation, meditation, yoga, guided imagery, and biofeedback.

Relaxation exercises and techniques are frequently included when behavioral problems are the focus of interventions because of their association with physiological arousal reduction that can have a negative influence on behavior (Novaco, 1975). The physiological arousal associated with aggression includes an increase in heart rate, muscle tension, and breathing rate (Kellner & Tuttin, 1995). With an increase in this physiological arousal comes an increase in angry thoughts, even more so when combined with alcohol and/or drugs, and results in an inhibition of internal control (Hollin, 2003). The ability to reduce the arousal response through increased self-regulation is a necessary ingredient in the prevention of an aggressive response. When adolescents were instructed in relaxation coping skills, they were able to calm down, to not become so angry in the first place, and to better think through and proactively cope with their angry feelings (Deffenbacher et al., 1996). According to the Margolin et al. (2002) study on male adolescent violence and aggression, these youth consistently reported angry thoughts as a trigger for the physical arousal that resulted in aggressive acts. These youth identified the instruction they had received in ameliorating the arousal by using relaxation techniques as an integral component in their ability to resist the subsequent impulsive, aggressive behaviors.

As previously noted, intervention programs in the area of aggression and anger management typically consist of a combination of components. Determining which of the components is efficacious is problematic because of the confounding effect of one element with another. Research on the efficacy of such individual elements has been recommended (Feindler & Ecton, 1986). For instance, Deffenbacher and Stark's (1992) study showed that relaxation coping skills were as effective in the treatment of anger as a combination of such skills with cognitive coping skills.

Purpose

In the proposed study, we will extend this previous research by assessing the effects of an isolated relaxation breathing exercise (RBE) applied to adolescent males in a juvenile justice residential program. Our study will employ an RBE in an attempt to (a) increase impulse control as indicated by measuring the frequency of use of curse words, (b) decrease the frequency of inappropriate behaviors as defined and measured by the juvenile justice behavior management system already in place at the facility, and (c) introduce self-monitoring of use of curse words, behavior, and use of the RBE. The purpose of this study is to determine the effect of an isolated RBE on both inappropriate behavior and language use in adolescents when practiced as an independent, single-component intervention.

Method

Participants

Six residents, ranging in age from 15 to 18, at a regional juvenile justice residential program will participate based on their being recommended by the program superintendent as requiring assistance with anger management and impulse control and on their having already been at the program for at least one month. At this facility, adolescent males satisfy court-ordered legal consequences for criminal behavior of a generally nonviolent nature. The reasons for each participant's placement in the justice program will be determined through brief interviews with each participant and corroborated by examining the information in the facility's files. These reasons will be summarized in the research report.

Informed consent will be obtained in writing from each of the six participants. Parental consent is not required, as the Florida Department of Juvenile Justice is considered to act in loco parentis by way of its approval of the study.

Design

The design of this study will be single subject with multiple baselines across six participants on two behavioral measures. The design designation is ABAB. Specifically, the initial baseline data-collection period with no treatment (Condition A) will last approximately 10 days. Then the RBE treatment (Condition B) will be introduced for 14 days. Following this, the RBE treatment will be withdrawn (Condition A) for 2 days. Finally, the RBE treatment will be reintroduced (Condition B) for at least 6 days. The use of two treatment phases will allow the researchers to observe any benefit that may result from the treatment and will increase the internal validity of the study.

Procedure

Independent variable. The researchers will instruct each participant in the practice of the RBE and tell participants on which day they should begin, stop, and begin again according to the ABAB design of the study described above.

The RBE treatment will follow a pattern of inhaling for the count of four, holding that breath for a count of seven, and exhaling for a count of eight, repeating the cycle five times (Weil, 1998). Participants will utilize the RBE at three points during the day: upon arising, at midday, and before going to sleep. Also, participants will use it at any point during the day when experiencing heightened feelings of anger or imminent loss of control over an impulsive response or outburst of aggression.

Fidelity of implementation. Fidelity of implementation will be indicated by participants' self-reports of the use of the RBE documented in their self-monitoring checklists. Specifically, each participant will be given an individualzed daily checklist to self-monitor compliance; the checklist will consist of an entry for each of the three times of day that the RBE must be used and for any additional times it is used. The checklists will be completed for each day by each of the participants.

Dependent Variables

Aggressive behavior scores. All residents at this facility will receive daily scores for behavior from 0% to 100%, with the higher score reflecting less aggression. Specifically, direct-care staff will observe residents throughout the day and mark checks on a daily log for various inappropriate behaviors, such as using curse words, being off task, and verbalizing or acting out hostility toward another resident or staff.

Inappropriate language scores. These scores will consist of daily checkmarks by direct-care staff for inappropriate language (curse words). This measure will indicate a specific type of lack of impulse control that often functions as a precursor to escalating aggressive behavior (Kellner, 1999).

Direct-care staff, who will record the daily checkmarks from which two types of scores are tabulated, will be trained by the director of the program's behavioral component. Throughout the course of any given period at the facility, two or more direct-care staff will be present. However, there may also be times, as when accompanying a resident from one building to the next, when only one staff member will be with a participant. These procedures are part of the regular program protocol and allow for continuous data collection by trained observers who will be present and collecting this data within the naturally occurring environment of the facility. To minimize impact, the researchers will visit the program only weekly during the course of the study after RBE is introduced to monitor participant compliance and to determine firsthand if any participant is experiencing problems, has any questions, or is no longer willing to continue in the study.

Participants will provide feedback on the daily behavior scores and use of inappropriate language reported by staff. Agreement between staff and participant judgment will be used as an indicator of reliability of the measures used in the study.

Analysis

Consistent with traditional reporting in single-subject research, the results will be reported separately for each of the six participants. For each participant, a line graph will be prepared for each of the two dependent variables. Figure 1 illustrates such a graph with *hypothetical* data for inappropriate language scores for one *hypothetical* participant.

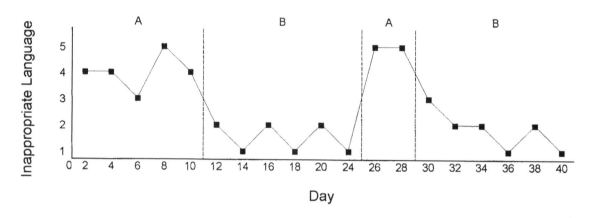
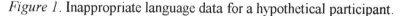

Figure 1. Inappropriate language data for a hypothetical participant.

Discussion

We will employ a relaxation breathing exercise (RBE) in an attempt to reduce anxiety while increasing impulse control and self-monitoring. We will take one frequent element of anger management (e.g., an RBE) and attempt to isolate its efficacy across six participants. This will help to determine the effectiveness of an RBE for use with male adolescents in residential juvenile justice programs.

Limitations

It is important to note that RBE will not be introduced to these participants without potential additional influences on their behavior. Additional factors that may influence results include additional social reinforcement for participating and prompting through the task of self-monitoring the use of the RBE. Self-report of compliance may provide a prompt to the participants to use the strategy. In addition, the researchers will visit the program once every week, spending several minutes with each participant individually, which may reinforce compliance.

We will employ participant self-report as both an attempt at self-monitoring and as an indicator of the reliability of staff-recorded behaviors on a daily basis. Future research efforts should attempt to increase reliability of measurement by having two independent observers record behavioral outcome measures in addition to participant self-report to check for self-monitoring.

Another limitation is due to the context of the project. The length of time available for the study will be limited by anticipated internal administrative changes at the facility. Therefore, our timeline will be relatively short.

References

Deffenbacher, J. L., Lynch, R. S., Oetting, E. R., & Kemper, C. C. (1996). Anger reduction in early adolescence. *Journal of Counseling Psychology, 2,* 149–157.

Deffenbacher, J. L., & Stark, R. S. (1992). Relaxation and cognitive-relaxation treatments of general anger. *Journal of Counseling Psychology, 39,* 158–167.

Feindler, E. L., & Ecton, R. B. (1986). *Adolescent anger control: Cognitive-behavioral techniques.* New York: Pergamon.

Fraser, M. W. (1996). Aggressive behavior in childhood and early adolescence: An ecological-developmental perspective on youth violence. *Social Work, 41,* 347–362.

Frey, K. S., Hirschstein, M. K., & Guzzo, B. A. (2000). Second Step: Preventing aggression by promoting social competence. *Journal of Emotional & Behavioral Disorders, 8*(2), 102–112.

Goldstein, A. P., Glick, B., & Gibbs, J. C. (1998). *Aggression replacement training (Rev. ed.).* Champaign, IL: Research Press.

Hollin, C. R. (2003). Aggression replacement training: Putting theory and research to work. *Reclaiming Children and Youth, 12*(3), 132–136.

Kazdin, A. E., Siegel, T. C., & Bass, D. (1992). Cognitive problem-solving skills training and parent management training in the treatment of antisocial behavior in children. *Journal of Consulting and Clinical Psychology, 60,* 733–747.

Kellner, M. H. (1999). The effects of anger management groups in a day school for emotionally disturbed adolescents. *Adolescence, 34,* 645–652.

Kellner, M. H., & Tuttin, J. (1995). A school-based anger management program for developmentally and emotionally disabled high school students. *Adolescence, 30,* 813–825.

Krug, E. G., Dahlberg, L. L., Mercy, J. A., Zwi, A. B., & Lozano, R. (Eds.). (2002). *World report on violence and health.* Geneva: World Health Organization.

Margolin, A., Youga, J., & Ballou, M. (2002). Voices of violence: A study of male adolescent aggression. *Journal of Humanistic Counseling, Education, and Development, 41,* 215–232.

Nietzel, M. T., Hasemann, D. M., & Lynam, D. R. (1999). Behavioral perspective on violent behavior. In V. B. Van Hasselt & M. Hersen (Eds.), *Handbook of psychological approaches with violent offenders: Contemporary strategies and issues* (pp. 39–66). New York: Kluwer Academic/Plenum.

Novaco, R. W. (1975). *Anger control: The development and evaluation of an experimental treatment.* Lexington, MA: D. C. Heath.

Rutherford, R. B. Jr., Quinn, M. M., & Mathur, S. A. (1996). *Effective strategies for teaching appropriate behaviors to children with emotional disorders/behavioral disorders.* Reston, VA: Council for Children with Behavioral Disorders. (ERIC Document Reproduction Service No. ED 391 304).

Snyder, K. W. (1999). Anger management for adolescents: Efficacy of brief group therapy. *Journal of the American Academy of Child and Adolescent Psychiatry, 38,* 1409–1420.

Snyder, S. N., & Sikmund, M. (1999). *Juvenile justice: A century of change.* (Juvenile Justice Clearinghouse Publication No. NCJ 178995). Rockville, MD: Office of Juvenile Justice and Delinquency Prevention.

Steiner, H., Garcia, I. G., & Matthews, Z. (1997). Posttraumatic stress disorder in incarcerated juvenile delinquents. *Journal of the American Academy of Child and Adolescent Psychiatry, 36,* 357–366.

Swenson, C. C., & Kennedy, W. A. (1995). Perceived control and treatment outcome with chronic adolescent offenders. *Adolescence, 30,* 565–579.

Weil, A. (1998). *Health and healing.* Shelburne, VT: Chapters.

Notes

Model Proposal 5: Quasi-Experimental Research

Intervening to Decrease Alcohol Abuse at University Parties: Differential Reinforcement of Intoxication Level[1]

A Research Proposal Based on the Work of

Angela K. Fournier

Ian J. Ehrhart

Kent E. Glindemann

E. Scott Geller

ABSTRACT

The quasi-experimental field study will assess whether an incentive/reward intervention can change the drinking behavior and the subsequent levels of intoxication among college students attending fraternity parties. A total of approximately 350 blood alcohol concentration (BAC) assessments, using hand-held breathalyzers, will be obtained at two baseline parties and at two intervention parties at the same fraternity house. At the intervention parties, the students will be informed they could win a cash prize if their BAC (Blood Alcohol Concentration) is below .05, and they will be given nomograms (charts that show how to calculate BAC from body weight, number of drinks consumed, and duration of a drinking bout) to aid in monitoring their levels of intoxication. It is predicted that mean BAC and the percentage of partiers with intoxication levels above .05 will be significantly lower at the two intervention parties than at the baseline parties.

Excessive alcohol consumption and binge drinking among college students continues to be a problem on campuses and in surrounding communities (e.g., Wechsler, Dowdall, Maenner, Gledhill-Hoyt, & Lee, 1998; Wechsler, Lee, Kuo, & Lee, 2000). Survey research reveals that 80% to 90% of all college students consume alcoholic beverages (Wechsler, Davenport, Dowdall, Moeykens, & Castillo, 1994). Excessive alcohol consumption and binge drinking often lead to a wide range of negative consequences. Such problems include poor academic and/or work performance, unplanned and/or unsafe sexual activity, sexual assault, property damage, physical violence, and vehicle crashes (e.g., Lewis, Malow, & Ireland, 1997; Meilman, 1993; Presley, Meilman, & Lyerla, 1993; Wechsler et al., 1998).

Among the college population, Greek-life students admit to consuming more alcoholic beverages per week, engaging in heavy drinking more often, and suffering more negative consequences than do their non-Greek-life peers (Cashin, Presley, & Meilman, 1998). Moreover, research assessing partygoers' actual blood alcohol concentration (BAC) levels found students at fraternity parties to get significantly more intoxicated than students at private parties, regardless of their Greek-life affiliation (Glindemann & Geller, 2003). Regardless of whether heavy drinkers

[1] This proposal was adapted from a report of completed research by Fournier, A. K., Ehrhart, I. J., Glindemann, K. E., & Geller, E. S. (2004). Intervening to decrease alcohol abuse at university parties: Differential reinforcement of intoxication level. *Behavior Modification, 28*, 167–181. Copyright © 2004 by Sage Publications, Inc. Reprinted with permission. Correspondence about the completed research may be addressed to Angela K. Fournier, Center for Applied Behavior Systems, Department of Psychology, Virginia Polytechnic Institute and State University, Blacksburg, VA 24061-0436. Electronic mail may be sent to akrom@vt.edu. The affiliations of the authors are: Angela K. Fournier, Ian J. Ehrhart, Kent E. Glindemann, and E. Scott Geller, Center for Applied Behavior Systems, Department of Psychology, Virginia Polytechnic Institute and State University.

are created by fraternities, drawn to fraternity membership, or attracted to fraternity parties, fraternities are a popular drinking environment and a socially valid setting for studying the efficacy of an innovative intervention approach.

Because a significant percentage of college students have alcohol-related problems, researchers and prevention practitioners have targeted this group with numerous intervention strategies, categorized as (a) legislation and enforcement, (b) education, (c) providing alternative activities, (d) promoting peer influence, and (e) environmental management. To date, these approaches have been met with modest and often disappointing results (Engs & Mulhall, 1981; Hansen & Graham, 1991). Systematic evaluations of intervention impact have been disappointing with regard to methodology. Although interventions using skills training, social norms, and harm reduction have resulted in lower levels of intoxication (e.g., Haines & Spear, 1997; Kivlahan, Marlatt, Fromme, Coppel, & Williams, 1990; Marlatt, 1996), these interventions were evaluated with self-report data rather than with observations of actual behavior or intoxication levels.

These self-reports are often in the form of interviews occurring up to 6 months after the actual drinking behavior. Furthermore, although comparisons of intoxication estimates and actual BAC have been significant (e.g., a Pearson r of .54 reported by Glindemann, Geller, & Ludwig, 1996), there is substantial room for error. It is anticipated that the current study will improve on these methodological limitations by using a physiological measure of alcohol intoxication (i.e., BAC).

The key component of the intervention evaluated in the research presented here is an incentive/reward contingency. An incentive is a verbal announcement (written or oral) of the availability of a positive consequence (reward) contingent on the occurrence of a certain behavior or an outcome of one or more behaviors. Partygoers in the present research will be informed of the availability of a monetary reward on meeting a particular BAC criterion. An immediate reward, in the form of a lottery ticket, will be given to all participants meeting the criterion.

Incentive/reward programs have been implemented to successfully improve various safety and health-related behaviors (Geller, 1993). More specifically, safety-belt use has been increased in numerous industrial settings and on college campuses. For example, during a campus-wide incentive/reward program, drivers observed using their shoulder belt had their vehicle license plate numbers recorded by campus police and entered into weekly prize raffles. Results showed dramatic increases in the target behavior, safety-belt use, during the incentive/reward condition (Rudd & Geller, 1985).

The incentive/reward intervention that will be evaluated in this proposed study is to differentially reinforce a behavioral outcome—BAC. The behavior of drinking alcohol is reinforced by the natural consequences of its use. Moderate levels of alcohol can elicit relaxation and facilitate social interaction, but high levels of alcohol can impair judgment and slow reaction time (Bailey, 1993). Thus, it appears the safe drinking of alcohol requires a certain degree of competency, which can be shaped through natural consequences. Differential reinforcement describes both natural and contrived environment-behavior contingencies and is critical for the development of individual performance skills (Skinner, 1953).

Operant conditioning (Skinner, 1957), particularly differential reinforcement, can be used to change a wide variety of behaviors. For example, the literature is abundant with studies using differential reinforcement to modulate drinking behavior. Much of the research has been conducted with animals, illustrating how operant conditioning can invoke and reduce drinking behavior (e.g., Black & Martin, 1972; DeNoble & Begleiter, 1976; Mello & Mendelson, 1965). These methods have also been successful with human drinking behavior as a means of treatment for alcohol dependence (e.g., Davidson & Bremser, 1977; Doyle & Samson, 1988; Sanders, Nathan, & O'Brien, 1976).

The target population for this proposed research—college students at fraternity parties—is not typically composed of individuals dependent on alcohol but often of students who abuse alcohol. Nevertheless, differential reinforcement will be used in an innovative way with the same objective: to lower BACs. Participants' levels of intoxication, a behavioral outcome of alcohol consumption, will be differentially reinforced. Specifically, participants will be rewarded for having a BAC lower than .05. Although operant conditioning has been used to treat alcohol abuse and dependence in humans, it has not been used in an applied setting such as a university fraternity party.

Upon entering an intervention party, partygoers will be told they can enter a cash raffle for $100 if their BAC at the end of the party is below .05 (i.e., .05 g of alcohol/deciliter of blood). The .05 BAC criterion has been chosen because of the dose-specific effects of alcohol neighboring this specific level of intoxication. Feelings of relaxation, lower inhibitions, and slight euphoria are characteristic of BACs ranging from .04 to .06 (Bailey, 1993) and are the effects students report desirable and motivating for alcohol consumption (Nezlek, Pilkington, & Bilbro, 1994; Orcutt, 1993; Wechsler et al., 1998). Once BACs of .05 or more are attained, impairment of psychomotor performance becomes likely (National Institute on Alcohol Abuse and Alcoholism, 1996).

For the intervention to be effective in lowering BACs, students will have to monitor their levels of intoxication and limit their alcohol consumption appropriately. Therefore, participants at the intervention parties will be given nomograms—charts that show how to calculate BAC from body weight, number of drinks consumed, and duration of a drinking bout. Nomograms have been used previously as prevention tools in several drunk-driving campaigns, but when used alone, they have not been very successful (Geller, 1990). For example, a study in a controlled drinking setting found prominent individual variation in BACs for given doses of alcohol (O'Neill, Williams, & Dubowski, 1983). The researchers concluded that alcohol nomograms could result in under- or overestimation of BACs and are not appropriate as single intervention tools for decreasing alcohol consumption. Therefore, nomograms will serve as an adjunct to the incentive/reward intervention in this proposed study, distributed to aid those students motivated to control their BAC.

Method

Participants and Settings

A total of approximately 500 college students will be asked to participate while attending one of four consecutive parties hosted by the same fraternity. It is anticipated that a majority of them will agree to participate. All four parties will take place between 10:00 P.M. and 2:00 A.M. during the next academic year. Each party will be held at the same off-campus fraternity house and will be open, meaning both Greek-life and non-Greek-life students can attend. All the parties will be relatively the same size, with 100 to 125 students in attendance. It is anticipated that less than 50% of the participants at each party will be fraternity members.

Materials and Apparatus

Participants' BACs will be assessed with hand-held Alco-Sensor IV breathalyzers (Intoximeters, Inc., St. Louis, MO). Prior to each BAC assessment, participants will remove residual alcohol by rinsing their mouths with 2 ounces of water. A standardized sampling procedure will be used to ensure alveolar (i.e., deep lung) air was collected. The local police department will calibrate all breathalyzers prior to each party.

Participants will be given flyers at the intervention parties as part of the incentive/reward intervention. Figure 1 illustrates the flyer that will be handed to all students at the intervention parties. The flyer will be 8.5 in. × 5.5 in. with black typewritten ink, informing students of the incentive/reward contingency. It will specify the following: (a) Researchers will give free BAC assessments at the end of the party; (b) those with a BAC below .05 will be entered in a $100 cash raffle; and (c) low intoxication can be maintained by snacking on food, consuming water between alcoholic beverages, and using the nomogram printed on the back of the flyer.

WIN $100 TONIGHT!

Virginia Tech researchers will be giving free BAC (blood alcohol concentration) assessments tonight.

If your BAC is **below .05**, you will be registered in a drawing for $100.

Here are some tips to help you keep a safe buzz:

- Drink a glass of water between each alcohol-containing drink.
- Snack on food before and while drinking.
- Use the attached chart to estimate a safe number of drinks for your body weight.

Figure 1. Flyer will be given to all students entering the intervention parties.

Figure 2 illustrates the gender-specific nomogram that will be attached to each flyer and distributed to all students at the intervention parties. The nomograms will be 6 in. × 3 in. white cards with black typewritten ink. In addition to information necessary to calculate approximate BAC, the nomograms will include instructions on how to use them, as well as information on how to interpret BACs (i.e., at a BAC of .08, an individual is legally intoxicated in Virginia).

MALE ALCOHOL IMPAIRMENT CHART
Approximate Blood Alcohol Percentage

Drinks	100	120	140	160	180	200	220	240	
0	.00	.00	.00	.00	.00	.00	.00	.00	ONLY SAFE DRIVING LIMIT
1	.04	.03	.03	.02	.02	.02	.02	.02	IMPAIRMENT
2	.08	.06	.05	.05	.04	.04	.03	.03	BEGINS
3	.11	.09	.08	.07	.06	.06	.05	.05	DRIVING SKILLS
4	.15	.12	.11	.09	.08	.08	.07	.06	SIGNIFICANTLY IMPAIRED
5	.19	.16	.13	.12	.11	.09	.09	.08	LEGALLY
6	.23	.19	.16	.14	.13	.11	.10	.09	INTOXICATED
7	.25	.22	.19	.16	.15	.13	.12	.11	CRIMINAL
8	.30	.25	.21	.19	.17	.15	.14	.13	PENALTIES
9	.34	.28	.24	.21	.19	.17	.15	.14	POSSIBLE DEATH AT
10	.38	.31	.27	.23	.21	.19	.17	.16	LOW BODY WEIGHT

Subtract 1 Drink for Every Hour of Drinking

1 drink = 1.5 oz. 80 proof liquor, 12 oz. beer, 5 oz. table wine

Figure 2. Nomogram will be attached to flyer and given to the males entering the intervention parties. The females will be given similar charts relevant to their gender.

Dependent Measures

The dependent measures will be mean BAC measured by hand-held breathalyzers, and the percentage of participants below certain criterion BAC levels—the raffle criterion (.05) and the legal limit of intoxication in Virginia (.08).

Data Collection

A systematic time-sampling procedure will be used to assess individual partygoers' BACs. Specifically, the research team will arrive at each party at 11:30 P.M. and collect BACs from participants for exactly 1 hour. The data-collection interval (11:30 P.M. to 12:30 A.M.) has been chosen because previous research in this environment indicated that this time interval allows for a representative sample of the partygoers' intoxication while maximizing the number of participants in the sample (Glindemann, Geller, & Fortney, 1999).

Once at the party, four teams of three research assistants each will be dispersed throughout the setting and station themselves in four distinct areas of the party. The research teams will be at the same four stations for each party. One researcher will recruit participants and obtain informed consent. Participant recruitment will be systematic and involve research assistants indiscriminately approaching students near their designated area of the party and requesting their participation. Researchers will attempt to recruit all students in their vicinity of the party.

Another researcher will assess participants' BACs and inform them of their intoxication level, in confidence. After receiving BAC feedback, participants will be warned not to drive if their BAC is greater than .05, encouraged not to consume any more alcohol if their BAC is greater than .08, and told they may experience serious negative consequences if they continue to drink when their BAC is greater than .15. As per fraternity policy, any students who appear to be intoxicated and at risk for dangerous alcohol-related problems will be reported to the fraternity's so-called sober crew.[2]

After they have received BAC feedback, participants' hands will be marked to avoid their being approached by a different research team in another area of the party. Hence, partygoers will be approached and allowed to have their BAC assessed only once. These methods have been approved by the human subjects review board and have proven effective for collecting relevant and representative data in previous studies (Geller, Kalsher, & Clarke, 1991; Glindemann et al., 1999; Glindemann & Geller, 2003).

Experimental Design and Conditions

This quasi-experimental field study will follow an A-A-B-B design, in which each A represents one baseline party and each B represents one intervention party. For the two baseline parties, research assistants will arrive at the fraternity party unannounced, collect data for 1 hour, then leave the party.

For the two intervention parties, which will follow the two baseline parties, two research assistants will arrive at the fraternity house at the start of the party (10:00 P.M.) and remain at the entrance to the fraternity house, handing a flyer and a nomogram to each attendant. As in the baseline condition, the four research teams will arrive at 11:30 P.M. and collect data for 1 hour. Participants meeting the raffle criterion will sign a raffle ticket and place it in a sealed box. At 12:30 A.M., one ticket will be drawn, and the winner will be announced to the party and immediately given a check for $100. Researchers will leave the party at that time.

---

[2] The sober crew is a group of selected fraternity members who remain sober throughout the party. In accordance with fraternity policy, these individuals are selected by the fraternity to monitor the party for unsafe behavior, including dangerous levels of intoxication.

Results

The mean BAC per party will be calculated. A two-condition (baseline vs. intervention) × two parties per condition × two Greek-life status (Greek-life vs. non-Greek-life) × two gender (men vs. women) analysis of variance (ANOVA) will be calculated on BAC.

In addition to the overall ANOVA, the BACs of Greek-life participants will be analyzed separately. Specifically, the mean BAC for Greek-life students at the baseline parties will be compared with the mean BAC for Greek-life students at the intervention parties for significance.

The percentage of participants below the .05 BAC level during the baseline parties and the percentage during the intervention parties will be calculated. The chi-square test will be used to determine the significance of the difference (i.e., percentage below .05 BAC at baseline parties versus percentage below .05 at intervention parties). Likewise, the percentage of participants below the .08 BAC level during the baseline parties and the percentage during the intervention parties will be calculated. The chi-square test will be used to determine the significance of the difference (i.e., percentage below .08 BAC at baseline parties versus percentage below .08 at intervention parties).

For all significance tests, an alpha level of $p < .05$ will be used.

Discussion

These findings will indicate the efficacy of the incentive/reward intervention to reduce intoxication levels at university-sanctioned fraternity parties.

One potential confound in this study is the possibility of a selection bias because of possible differential participation of the moderate or nondrinking partygoers. These students may not be motivated to participate in the baseline BAC assessments because there will be no reward for a low BAC, and the BAC feedback will be relatively inconsequential. The extent of this potential bias is low, however, because the research teams will indiscriminately approach students at each party. More important, those with relatively high BACs rarely refuse a BAC assessment (cf. Geller et al., 1991; Glindemann et al., 1999; Glindemann et al., 1996).

Another area of concern may be a sampling bias at the entrance to the party. Heavy-drinking students might be discouraged and leave the party immediately when receiving a flyer, prompting low BACs. It is anticipated, however, that this will not happen. The research assistants located at the only entrance and exit to the party will hand flyers to everyone entering the house and will observe anyone leaving the party after receiving a flyer. These researchers will be present from the start of the party until the end of data collection, increasing the length of time researchers will be at the party. One may suspect that the mere presence of researchers at the entrance could impact drinking behavior. However, the researchers will be unobtrusively dressed in casual clothing, similar to partygoers, and stand next to fraternity members who will be checking guests' identification and collecting entrance fees. They will not be identifiable as researchers and will remain separate from the rest of the researchers once they arrive.

History effects are another potential confound. With the A-A-B-B design and with no control group, it is possible that something other than the intervention will occur between baseline and intervention parties to affect BACs. However, researchers will track all alcohol-related interventions and current events at fraternity, university, and community levels and note any changes that would affect college alcohol consumption. The same fraternity house will be used throughout the study, and therefore, the environmental context will be consistent. Although partygoers will vary across parties, the mean age, gender mix, and proportion of fraternity members at each party will be measured, and it is anticipated that these will be quite stable.

Just the availability of a BAC contingency should lower the level of intoxication expected at a party. In fact, this could be a most effective and acceptable way to change campus norms with regard to alcohol consumption. The incentive/reward contingency should give partygoers an excuse to consume less alcohol and allow them an opportunity to experience the natural reinforcers accompanying lower intoxication levels. Multiple exposures to the incentive/reward contingency could influence a significant percentage of partygoers to consume less alcohol at future parties that do not apply the intervention.

In summary, the incentive/reward intervention has the potential to be a simple, socially valid approach to reducing college alcohol abuse that is potentially effective for large-scale application. This field study will be the first to demonstrate the efficacy of differential reinforcement in controlling student intoxication in a party setting, and the potential for the incentive/reward intervention to be self-supported makes it feasible for adoption by university policy.

References

Bailey, W. J. (1993). *Drug use in American society* (3rd ed.). Minneapolis, MN: Burgess.

Black, E. L., & Martin, G. L. (1972). Extinction of alcohol drinking in rats following acquisition of a fixed-ratio schedule of reinforcement. *Psychonomic Science, 29*, 152–154.

Cashin, J. R., Presley, C. A., & Meilman, P. W. (1998). Alcohol use in the Greek-life system: Follow the leader? *Journal of Studies on Alcohol, 59*, 63–70.

Davidson, R. S., & Bremser, R. F. (1977). Controlled alcoholic drinking: Differential reinforcement of low rates of drinking. *Behavior Modification, 1*, 221–233.

DeNoble, V., & Begleiter, H. (1976). Response suppression on a mixed schedule of reinforcement during alcohol withdrawal. *Pharmacology, Biochemistry & Behavior, 5*, 227–229.

Doyle, T. F., & Samson, H. H. (1988). Adjunctive alcohol drinking in humans. *Physiology & Behavior, 44*, 775–779.

Engs, R. C., & Mulhall, P. F. (1981). Again let's look before we leap: The effects of physical activity on smoking and drinking patterns. *Journal of Alcohol and Drug Education, 26*, 65–74.

Geller, E. S. (1990). Preventing injuries and deaths from vehicle crashes: Encouraging belts and discouraging booze. In J. Edwards, R. S. Tindale, L. Heath, & E. J. Posavac (Eds.), *Social influence processes and prevention* (pp. 249–277). New York: Plenum.

Geller, E. S. (1993). Increasing road safety behaviors. In D. S. Glenwick & L. A. Jason (Eds.), *Promoting health and mental health in children, youth, and families* (pp. 149–177). New York: Springer.

Geller, E. S., Kalsher, M. J., & Clarke, S. W. (1991). Beer versus mixed-drink consumption at university parties: A time and place for low alcohol alternatives. *Journal of Studies on Alcohol, 52*, 197–204.

Glindemann, K. E., & Geller, E. S., (2003). A systematic assessment of intoxication at university parties: Effects of the environmental context. *Environment & Behavior, 5*, 655–664.

Glindemann, K. E., Geller, E. S., & Fortney, J. N. (1999). Self-esteem and alcohol consumption: A study of college drinking behavior in a naturalistic setting. *Journal of Alcohol and Drug Education, 45*, 60–71.

Glindemann, K. E., Geller, E. S., & Ludwig, T. D. (1996). Behavioral intentions and blood alcohol concentration: A relationship for prevention intervention. *Journal of Alcohol and Drug Education, 41*, 120–134.

Haines, M., & Spear, S. F. (1997). Changing the perception of the norm: A strategy to decrease binge drinking among college students. *Journal of American College Health, 45*, 134–140.

Hansen, W. B., & Graham, J. W. (1991). Preventing alcohol, marijuana, and cigarette use among adolescents: Peer pressure resistance training versus establishing conservative norms. *Preventive Medicine, 15*, 363–372.

Kivlahan, D. R., Marlatt, G. A., Fromme, K., Coppel, D. B., & Williams, E. (1990). Secondary prevention with college drinkers: Evaluation of an alcohol skills training program. *Journal of Consulting and Clinical Psychology, 58*, 805–810.

Lewis, J. E., Malow, R. M., & Ireland, S. J. (1997). HIV/AIDS risk in heterosexual college students: A review of a decade of literature. *Journal of American College Health, 45*, 147–157.

Marlatt, G. A. (1996). Reducing college student binge drinking: A harm-reduction approach. In R. J. Resnick & R. H. Rozensky (Eds.), *Health psychology throughout the life span: Practice and research opportunities* (pp. 377–392). Washington, DC: American Psychological Association.

Meilman, P. W. (1993). Alcohol-induced sexual behavior on campus. *Journal of American College Health, 42*, 27–31.

Mello, N. K., & Mendelson, J. H. (1965). Operant drinking of alcohol on a rate-contingent ratio schedule of reinforcement. *Journal of Psychiatric Research, 3*, 145–152.

National Institute on Alcohol Abuse and Alcoholism. (1996). *Alcohol alert* (No. 3IPH362). Washington, DC: National Institutes of Health.

Nezlek, J. B., Pilkington, C. J., & Bilbro, J. G. (1994). Moderation in excess: Binge drinking and social interaction among college students. *Journal of Studies on Alcohol, 55*, 342–351.

O'Neill, B., Williams, A. F., & Dubowski, K. M. (1983). Variability in blood alcohol concentrations: Implications for estimating individual results. *Journal of Studies on Alcohol, 44*, 222–230.

Orcutt, J. D. (1993). Happy hour and social lubrication: Evidence on mood-setting rituals of drinking time. *Journal of Drug Issues, 23*, 389–407.

Presley, C. A., Meilman, P. W., & Lyerla, R. (1993). *Alcohol and other drugs on American college campuses: Use, consequences, and perceptions of the campus environment* (Vol. I: 1989–1991). Carbondale: Southern Illinois University at Carbondale.

Rudd, J. R., & Geller, E. S. (1985). A university-based incentive program to increase safety-belt use: Toward cost-effective institutionalization. *Journal of Applied Behavior Analysis, 18*, 215–226.

Sanders, R. M., Nathan, P. E., & O'Brien, J. S. (1976). The performance of adult alcoholics working for alcohol: A detailed operant analysis. *British Journal of Addiction, 71*, 307–319.

Skinner, B. F. (1953). *Science and human behavior.* New York: Macmillan.

Skinner, B. F. (1957). *Schedules of reinforcement.* New York: Macmillan.

Wechsler, H., Davenport, A. E., Dowdall, G., Moeykens, M., & Castillo, S. (1994). Health and behavioral consequences of binge drinking in college: A national survey of students at 140 campuses. *Journal of the American Medical Association, 272*, 1672–1677.

Wechsler, H., Dowdall, G. W., Maenner, G., Gledhill-Hoyt, J., & Lee, H. (1998). Changes in binge drinking and related problems among American college students between 1993 and 1997: Results of the Harvard School of Public Health college alcohol study. *Journal of American College Health, 47*, 57–66.

Wechsler, H., Lee, J. E., Kuo, M., & Lee, H. (2000). College binge drinking in the 1990s: A continuing problem. *Journal of American College Health, 48*, 199–210.

Model Proposal 6: True Experiment

Traits and Behaviors Assigned to an Adolescent Wearing an Alcohol Promotional T-Shirt[1]

A Research Proposal Based on the Work of

Jane E. Workman   Naomi E. Arseneau

Chandra J. Ewell

ABSTRACT

The purpose of this study is to examine meanings assigned by observers to an adolescent wearing an alcohol promotional T-shirt. Approximately 50 male and 50 female university students will record their impressions of a male or female adolescent wearing an alcohol T-shirt or a plain T-shirt for 14 traits (healthy, athletic, trustworthy, sociable, fashionable, feminine, independent, masculine, relaxed, responsible, honest, attractive, reliable, and religious). They will also rate 14 behaviors (be on time for work/class, smoke cigarettes, be violent, do well in school, use illegal drugs, be a loser, be a member of the "in" crowd, be a party animal, drink alcohol, be a risk taker, get drunk, be a sports fan, be a good friend, and use profanity). Gender differences will be explored. This study will have implications for Havighurst's (1953) theory of developmental tasks and Livesley and Bromley's (1973) impression formation theory. In addition, it will have practical and policy implications.

Clothing functions as a symbol to which meanings are assigned by wearer, observer, or both (Darden & Worden, 1991). Promotional T-shirts, imprinted with an alcohol brand name, have communication potential from the perspective of both wearer and observer. The messages communicated by the wearer may or may not be accurately interpreted by the observer. Interpretation of the messages may rely on stereotypes conveyed by the mass media. For example, alcohol advertisements create images of alcohol users who are independent, attractive, sociable, and risk takers. These images are stereotypes that may become embedded in an individual's subconscious; the images are activated when the subconscious is triggered by a cue such as an alcohol advertisement on a promotional T-shirt (Livesley & Bromley, 1973). The images may be especially appealing to adolescents because of their relationship to the developmental tasks of adolescence. For example, being sociable is important to achievement of the developmental tasks of forming close friendships and becoming integrated into a peer group (Klaczynski, 1990). An essential component of normal adolescent development is experimentation with a wide range of behaviors (Irwin, 1993), some of which may be risky behaviors; for example, experimenting with alcohol.

---

[1] This proposal was adapted from a report of completed research by Workman, J. E., Arseneau, N. E., & Ewell, C. J. (2004). Traits and behaviors assigned to an adolescent wearing an alcohol promotional t-shirt. *Family and Consumer Sciences Research Journal, 33*, 62–80. Copyright © 2004 by the American Association of Family and Consumer Sciences. Reprinted with permission. Correspondence about the completed research may be addressed to Jane E. Workman, 311H Quigley Hall, Architecture & Interior Design MC 4318, Southern Illinois University, Carbondale, IL 62901. Electronic mail may be sent to jworkman@siu.edu. The affiliations of the authors are: Jane E. Workman, Naomi E. Arseneau, and Chandra J. Ewell, Southern Illinois University, Carbondale.

Review of Related Literature

Adolescent Traits and Behaviors

A classic conception of adolescence characterizes it as consisting of two stages: early adolescence (ages 12 to 18) and late adolescence (ages 18 to 22) (Erikson, 1963, 1982, 1997). During early adolescence, physical maturation, emotional development, peer group membership, and heterosexual relationships are developmental tasks, whereas the developmental tasks of later adolescence revolve around autonomy from parents, sex role identity, internalized morality, and career choices (Newman & Newman, 1987).

Risk taking was used as a perspective to delineate adolescent traits and behaviors and to explain the choices being made by adolescents. Risk taking includes deliberately chosen behaviors with uncertain, and possibly negative, outcomes (Irwin, 1993). Increased risk taking is typical of normal adolescent development (Baumrind, 1987). For example, learning to take initiative, a developmental task of adolescence, may involve taking risks (Baumrind, 1987).

The high incidence of risky behavior during adolescence is sometimes attributed to cognitive immaturity, with the assumption that adults are more sensitive to the potential consequences of their actions than adolescents (Bell & Bell, 1993). However, Gardner (1993) proposed that reckless decisions could in some instances be rational. For example, risk taking may be a way of coping with a perceived lack of personal control over an environment viewed as mainly controlled by adults (Lyng, 1990). The meanings, motivations, and consequences of risk taking may differ for women and men (Anderson et al., 1993).

Gardner (1993) speculated that adolescents not only make more impulsive decisions than adults but also rationalize their impulsive choices by downplaying the personal risk. Adolescents who can regulate their behavior or remove themselves from tempting situations have an advantage in resisting risky situations (Gardner, 1993).

Adolescent Norms: Clothing, Gender, and Alcohol

O'Neal (1998) investigated why adolescents engaged in risky behaviors related to dress. Based on focus group interviews with 300 adolescents in Grades 9 through 12, O'Neal concluded that students made rational decisions to wear dress that had the potential for negative outcomes (physical abuse) to avoid other negative outcomes (social and emotional abuse). Social and emotional abuse such as isolation, intimidation, humiliation, and other forms of peer discrimination were considered by the students to be more likely negative outcomes than physical abuse. Adolescent risk taking relative to dress may be an example of using dress decisions to cope with a perceived lack of personal control. Gardner (1993) speculated that adolescents who rationalized their reckless choices by downplaying personal risk may have downplayed the probability of physical risk while emphasizing social and emotional benefits.

Many developmental tasks can be facilitated or hindered by clothing choices—for example, becoming integrated into a peer group or acquiring individuality. In evaluating the self and others, adolescents tend to use appearance standards (Kaiser, 1997). "Although such comparisons and assessments occur throughout the life cycle, they are likely to be especially acute in the transitional period of adolescence, when the need to belong is combined with a strong emphasis on appearance concerns" (Kaiser, 1997, p. 354). Clothing is a visible means by which adolescents express both conformity and individuality (MacGillivray & Wilson, 1997). There is some evidence that conformity to peer expectations in dress enhances social acceptability and opportunities for social interaction (Workman & Johnson, 1994).

Based on observation and interviews of high school students, Eicher, Baizerman, and Michelman (1991) concluded that adolescents were conscious of their own dress and their peers' dress. Furthermore, adolescents differentiated peer groups by their dress. Indeed, these authors suggested that groups with extreme dress provided a standard against which an adolescent could compare himself or herself.

Suitor and colleagues (Suitor & Carter, 1999; Suitor, Minyard, & Carter, 2001; Suitor & Reavis, 1995) conducted several studies to investigate adolescent gender norms. Suitor and colleagues reasoned that adolescents adhere to group norms as a means to acquire prestige; therefore, the norms that exist in a particular group can be uncovered by looking at the methods by which group members acquire prestige. Prestige is an individual's position in a status hierarchy (Kaiser, 1997). In each study, to measure adolescent norms, college students listed five ways in which males and five ways in which females gained prestige in the high schools they attended. Suitor and colleagues concluded that except for an increase in sports as a way for girls to gain prestige, adolescent gender norms did not seem to have changed during the past 40 years. Dress and appearance were among the top seven means of adhering to gender norms and thereby gaining prestige. Girls gained prestige primarily through physical attractiveness, sociability, academic achievement, popularity with the opposite sex, clothes, participation in school activities, and cheerleading. Boys gained prestige primarily through sports, academic achievement, access to cars, sociability, popularity with the opposite sex, physical attractiveness, and participation in school activities. Boys were more likely than girls to gain prestige through risky behaviors, such as fighting or using drugs and alcohol. Indeed, using drugs or alcohol ranked 9th among ways boys gained prestige and 13th among ways girls gained prestige. A desire for prestige and social acceptance can influence many types of decisions—for example, the decision to use or not use alcohol.

Barnett and Miller (2001) reported on adolescents' motivations to use or not use alcohol. A norm was defined as "an individual's behaviors that are motivated by some guideline or standard" (Barnett & Miller, 2001, p. 209). Descriptive norms are what people usually do, whereas "personal norms are internalized values and expectations for one's own behavior, regardless of external reward or imposition by others" (Barnett & Miller, 2001, p. 209). Participants in Barnett and Miller's study, with a mean age of 13, reported personal norms as one reason for not using alcohol. For example, personal norms were reflected in responses that he or she was not the kind of person who drinks, that others know not to offer alcohol to him or her, and that he or she does not act like he or she wants to drink. Descriptive norms related to alcohol use included the following: to fit in, to be popular, to be cool, to acquire friends, to gain attention, and to have fun. Adhering to norms as a means to gain social acceptance (i.e., popularity, prestige) was a key motivation in the decision to use or not use alcohol.

Alcohol commercials have been criticized because the images of alcohol users parallel the images many adolescents try to fashion for themselves (Fox, Krugman, Fletcher, & Fischer, 1998). Perhaps the images appeal to adolescents because they are intimately related to many of the personal traits and behaviors associated with successful achievement of the developmental tasks of adolescence.

Personal Traits Associated with Alcohol Use

Social, relaxed, independent, attractive. Alcohol advertising creates images of alcohol users who are young, attractive, sexy, independent, relaxed, sociable, and successful (Brown, Parks, Zimmerman, & Phillips, 2001; Domzal & Kernan, 1992; Kropp, Lavack, & Holden, 1999; Mosher, 1994; Parker, 1998; Strasburger, 1995). For example, Waiters, Treno, and Grube (2001) found that one main message of alcohol commercials seemed to be social success; as noted by one student, "If you drink it, then you can go to parties and be cool" (p. 708).

Healthy. Adolescent alcohol abuse has been identified as the top public health problem in the United States (Robert Wood Johnson Foundation, 2001). Health problems associated with adolescent drinking include sleep difficulties, chest discomfort, abdominal complaints, muscle and joint pain, headaches, elevated liver enzyme levels, motor vehicle accidents, violent crime, elevated risk factors during adulthood for alcohol dependence and drug abuse, fighting, stealing, depression, suicide, and absenteeism from school or work (Gillmore et al., 1998; Komro &

Toomey, 2002; Mosher, 1994; "Researchers Find Health Problems," 2001). Conversely, alcohol advertisements depict beer as nutritious, healthy, and natural (Domzal & Kernan, 1992; Waiters et al., 2001). Indeed, Waiters et al. (2001) found that 9- to 15-year-old students interpreted advertisements to mean that "drinkers would enjoy health benefits, become capable of strenuous physical activity, become better athletes, or enjoy improved overall well-being" (p. 711).

Feminine, masculine. Gender roles are among developmental tasks usually internalized by early adolescence. Research has found gender differences in interpretation and appeal of alcohol advertisements (Andsager, Austin, & Pinkleton, 2002; Covell, 1992; Covell, Dion, & Dion, 1994; Kelly & Edwards, 1998). For example, Andsager et al. (2002) found that boys and girls (578 9th- and 12th-grade students) interpreted eight alcohol-related messages differently. The authors suggested that gender should be a variable included in models seeking to explain how adolescents analyze messages.

Fashionable. Abercrombie & Fitch Company has coupled alcohol and fashion with its catalog-magazine, the *A&F Quarterly* ("Du-ude! Clothiers Catalog," 1998). The catalog contains the expected—advertisements for Abercrombie's casual wear—and the unexpected—features such as a page titled "Drinking 101." Indeed, it is common practice for alcohol advertisements to feature fashionable models that are young, sexy, successful, active, and attractive (Strasburger, 1995).

Trustworthy, responsible, reliable, honest. In an effort to associate drinking with responsible behavior, alcohol marketers have undertaken campaigns promoting responsible drinking, for example, "Think When You Drink," "Drink Safely," and "Know When to Say When" (Treise, Wolburg, & Otnes, 1999). It is widely acknowledged that alcohol use contributes to untrustworthy, irresponsible, unreliable, and dishonest behavior.

Athletic. Peretti-Watel, Beck, and Legleye (2002) found a significant link between participation in team sports and alcohol use (for both genders) or recent drunkenness (for boys). These authors considered sociability as an important factor in the link between sports and alcohol. The results are consistent with relationships shown between sporting activities, violence, and risky behaviors (Thorlindsson, 2001).

Religious. Religious commitment is one variable that has been shown to be related to risky behavior among adolescents (Jeynes, 2001). Religious commitment has been found to be associated with higher educational outcomes and a lower incidence of alcohol abuse (Mason & Windle, 2001; Miller, Davies, & Greenwald, 2000). For example, Mason and Windle (2001) collected data from students attending a suburban school district and found that decreased alcohol use was associated with variables measuring religiosity, school grades, and peer alcohol use.

Miller et al. (2000) surveyed adolescents to examine the relationship between substance abuse and religiosity. Religiosity was assessed through affiliation with a religious denomination and through response to seven questions concerning belief and practice. Personal devotion (a personal relationship with the Divine), affiliation with fundamentalist religious denominations, and personal conservatism (a personal commitment to teaching and living according to creed) were all inversely associated with alcohol use. Miller et al. concluded that low levels of religiosity may be associated with adolescent alcohol use and abuse.

Behaviors Associated with Alcohol Use

Smoking, illegal drug use, alcohol abuse, violence. Tobacco and alcohol use are correlated with one another, as well as with other risky behaviors (Johnston, O'Malley, & Bachman, 1987; Parker, 1998). For example, alcohol use is associated with drug abuse, motor vehicle crashes, and violent crime (Simons-Morton et al., 1999).

Risk taker. Kuther and Higgins-D'Alessandro (2000) studied the relations among risky behaviors, moral reasoning, and domain judgment by comparing students in an alternative school with students from the high school with which it was associated. Risky behaviors were primarily perceived to be within the domain of personal decisions rather than moral or conventional ones. With increasing alcohol use, students were more likely to view the decision to use alcohol as a personal decision rather than as either a moral or conventional decision. Adolescents may view their decision to engage in risky behavior as their own business and refuse to acknowledge the consequences of their behavior for other people.

Academic achievement. A report by the American Medical Association compiled from 60 recent studies concluded that alcohol use by adolescents can cause damage to their learning and memory (Kotulak, 2002). Even after three weeks of not drinking, the brains of adolescents who regularly drank alcohol functioned 10% less than normal in ability to learn and retain new information. A 10% reduction in the ability to learn and retain new information could have a measurable effect on academic achievement—for example, passing or failing a course. Indeed, other research has found a relationship between drinking and problems with cognitive impairment and academic performance (Hanson & Engs, 1992).

Mathios, Avery, Bisogni, and Shanahan (1998) did a content analysis of alcohol messages embedded in prime-time television programs. Personality characteristics were coded using three adjective pairs: smart/stupid, admirable/despicable, and powerful/powerless. Personality traits of adolescent characters consuming alcohol were primarily negative (i.e., stupid, despicable, powerless) whereas traits of adult and high-income characters consuming alcohol were primarily positive (i.e., smart, admirable, powerful). Adults and high-income characters, ostensible role models for adolescents, were portrayed with positive linkages to alcohol consumption.

Member of the in-crowd or a loser. Santor, Messervey, and Kusumakar (2000) speculated that the need to be popular was related to conformity to peer group norms. Substance use and risk-taking behavior may represent efforts to conform to group norms. Need to be popular was measured by 12 items—for example, "I'd do almost anything to avoid being seen as a loser," "I've gone to parties just to be part of the crowd," and "I often do things just to be popular with people at school." Santor et al. found need to be popular was positively correlated with beer drinking.

Party animal. Spuds MacKenzie, the "Original Party Animal" in commercials for Bud Light, embodied the popular notion of a link between alcohol and partying (Mitchell, 1989; Traux, 1990). Wallack, Grube, Madden, and Breed (1990) found that almost 60% of 468 5th- and 6th-grade students could identify Spuds MacKenzie and more than 80% could match him with Budweiser beer—9 times the number who could identify a Coca-Cola slogan. Martino (1999) confirmed that the label "party animals" applied to students who had a reputation for getting drunk at parties.

Sports fan. Madden and Grube (1994) examined frequency and nature of alcohol advertising in a random sample of televised sports events. More commercials occurred for alcohol products than for any other beverage, with beer commercials predominating. In addition to commercials, alcohol advertising appeared on stadium signs, on-site promotions, and product sponsorships. Madden and Grube concluded that sports fans received primarily positive messages about drinking.

Be a good friend. Advertisements portray good friends drinking together in social situations and emphasize the ability of alcohol to enhance friendship—for example, "Beer is about friendship" (Treise et al., 1999, p. 23). Public service announcements use the association of alcohol and friendship to promote such campaigns as "Friends don't let friends drive drunk" (Treise et al., 1999).

Use profanity. Alcohol is known to release inhibitions and provoke aggression and hostility (Treise et al., 1999). Hostile and profane language, language that might be restrained in other contexts, is one facet of hostile behavior.

Theoretical Background

The theoretical background for this study is composed of two theories: Havighurst's (1953) theory of developmental tasks and Livesley and Bromley's (1973) impression formation theory. A developmental task is

> a task which arises at or about a certain period in the life of the individual, successful achievement of which leads to happiness and to success with later tasks, while failure leads to unhappiness in the individual, disapproval by the society, and difficulty with later tasks. (Havighurst, 1953, p. 2)

Developmental tasks arising during adolescence include gaining autonomy from parents, forming close friendships, acquiring individuality, becoming integrated into a peer group, developing a realistic self-perception, creating a separate identity, and cultivating sociopolitical awareness (Havighurst, 1953; Silbereisen, Eyferth, & Rudinger, 1986).

Developmental tasks of adolescence revolve around development of the self. The self is intimately linked to appearance—"the self is established, maintained, and altered in social transactions as much by the communications of appearance as by discourse" (Stone, 1981, p. 102). Dress and appearance are visible indicators of successful achievement of many developmental tasks, such as development of personal traits related to peer group integration (e.g., sociability, independence) or behaviors related to peer group norms (e.g., risk taking, party animal). Adolescents can use dress (e.g., message T-shirts) to condone attitudes, behaviors, beliefs, values, and group affiliations that simultaneously communicates their identity, autonomy, peer group integration, sociopolitical awareness, individuality, and self-perception.

Impression formation theory provided the context within which to look at impressions of an adolescent based on what he or she is wearing. According to impression formation theory, observers form impressions of others in four stages: cue selection, interpretative inference, extended inference, and anticipatory set (Livesley & Bromley, 1973, pp. 16–17). All stages of the process of impression formation are influenced by characteristics of the observer (e.g., age, gender), characteristics of the specific cues selected (e.g., alcohol T-shirt, plain T-shirt), characteristics of the person being observed (e.g., age, gender), as well as relationships between the observer and the observed (e.g., strangers, friends, acquaintances).

In the first stage, cue selection, out of the variety of cues available, an observer selects specific cues (Livesley & Bromley, 1973, p. 16). Because clothing is visible even if no words are exchanged, clothing can consciously or unconsciously become the selected cue that is a basis for formation of impressions. For example, an adolescent may notice that one of his or her peers is wearing an alcohol promotional T-shirt.

In the second stage, interpretative inference, the observer uses the cues selected in the first stage to form impressions of general traits—for example, personality traits or intelligence (Livesley & Bromley, 1973, p. 16). Appearance cues affect the impressions made—impressions that may be accurate or inaccurate. In the case of an alcohol promotional T-shirt, it is unknown what general traits are associated with the cue; but based on the review of literature, it can be speculated that relaxed and sociable might be among the traits.

In the third stage, extended inference, the observer forms impressions of additional personal traits as well as impressions that extend beyond personal traits (Livesley & Bromley, 1973, p. 16). Impressions might extend to such features as, for example, whether the person smokes, likes to party, or is willing to take risks, or whether the adolescent's parents are lenient or strict.

In the fourth stage, anticipatory set, the observer integrates all the previous impressions and forms an overall impression that becomes a basis for interaction (Livesley & Bromley, 1973, p. 17). Contextual factors affect perception, that is, the meaning of a cue varies with the situation. An alcohol promotional T-shirt worn in a public school setting might produce different impressions from those of the same T-shirt worn to a sporting event. Stereotypes associated with some appearance features give clues about how a person is likely to behave (Livesley & Bromley, 1973, p. 21). Accurate or inaccurate, the observer uses the impressions he or she has made to decide whether to interact with the other person and, if the decision is to interact, then how to approach him or her—for example, by attempting to "bum" a cigarette, offer him or her a drink, or invite him or her to a drinking party.

Purpose of the Study

The purpose of this proposed study is to examine meanings assigned by observers to an adolescent wearing an alcohol promotional T-shirt. This study will examine variations in characteristics of the specific cues (i.e., alcohol T-shirt, plain T-shirt) and variations in characteristics of the person being observed (i.e., male, female) while maintaining age of observed as a constant (i.e., peers, later adolescence). Within the framework of the process of impression formation, the study will also examine variations in characteristics of the observer (i.e., male, female). The relationship between the observers and the observed (i.e., strangers) will be a constant.

Based on the review of literature, the theory of developmental tasks and impression formation theory, the following null hypotheses are proposed. Hypotheses 1 and 2 are based on the literature presented showing associations between personal traits and behaviors and alcohol use:

Null hypothesis 1: There will be no significant difference in impressions of an adolescent's personal traits based on type of T-shirt (plain vs. alcohol promotional).

Null hypothesis 2: There will be no significant difference in impressions of an adolescent's expected behaviors based on type of T-shirt (plain vs. alcohol promotional).

Hypotheses 3, 4, 5, and 6 are based on Livesley and Bromley's (1973) theory of impression formation as well as research by Andsager et al. (2002), Covell (1992), Covell et al. (1994), and Kelly and Edwards (1998). All these authors suggest that gender should be a variable investigated when trying to explain how adolescents analyze messages.

Null hypothesis 3: There will be no significant difference in impressions of an adolescent's personal traits based on gender.

Null hypothesis 4: There will be no significant difference in impressions of an adolescent's expected behaviors based on gender.

Null hypothesis 5: There will be no interaction between gender of wearer and type of T-shirt on impressions of an adolescent's personal traits or expected behaviors.

Null hypothesis 6: There will be no interaction between gender of observer and type of T-shirt on impressions of an adolescent's personal traits or expected behaviors.

Method

Materials and Instruments

Two Caucasian adolescents (one male, one female, both age 19) will be photographed wearing T-shirts with and without an alcohol brand name. Every effort will be made to ensure that all other aspects of the photographs are the same (e.g., posture, facial expression, background). The background will be a set of lockers to establish the context as a school setting. Each adolescent will be photographed reaching up to an opened locker door.

Items will measure impressions of the adolescent for 14 personal traits and 14 behaviors (see Tables 1–4, which list traits and behaviors). Personal traits and behaviors were chosen to be reflective of traits and behaviors associated with alcohol users reported in the literature. Each trait will be rated on a 7-point bipolar scale (e.g., healthy-not healthy, religious-not religious). Each behavior will be accompanied by a 7-point scale (7 = *likely* and 1 = *not likely*). Some filler items[2] will be included to obscure the true purpose of the study.

Procedure

Folders will be randomly distributed to participants in classroom situations. Each participant will receive a folder with one photograph (a male wearing an alcohol T-shirt, or a male wearing a plain T-shirt, or a female wearing an alcohol T-shirt, or a female wearing a plain T-shirt), a copy of the impression formation items, and a sheet on which to record demographic information. After reading an introductory paragraph,[3] each participant will record his or her impressions of the person in the photograph for 14 personal traits and 18 behaviors. Then participants will complete the demographic information. The study will take about 10 to 15 minutes to complete.

Participants

Participants will be approximately 50 male and 50 female university students, distributed among 27 different majors, and will include freshmen, sophomores, juniors, and seniors. Based on the demographics of the university's students, it is anticipated that the vast majority of participants in the sample will be Caucasian, with a small percentage being African Americans, Asians, and other ethnicities. Also, almost all participants will be single and will belong to the middle-middle to upper-middle social classes.

Analysis

A mean will be computed for personal traits for each group of participants (i.e., a mean for the group viewing an alcohol T-shirt and a mean for the group viewing a plain T-shirt). These means, along with the results of ANOVA (i.e., F test) will be presented in a table such as Table 1 below.

Table 1

Results for Personal Traits Based on Alcohol T-Shirt versus Plain T-Shirt

Trait	Mean for alcohol T-shirt	Mean for plain T-shirt	F	p
Healthy				
Athletic				
Trustworthy				
Sociable				
Fashionable				
Feminine				
Independent				
Masculine				
Relaxed				
Responsible				
Honest				
Attractive				
Reliable				
Religious				

Note. Mean scores based on a 7-point bipolar scale (7 = *healthy* and 1 = *not healthy*)

---

[2] Filler items will include cheat on an exam, gossip, tell a lie, and obey the speed limit.

[3] "According to Dr. Leonard Zunin, 'four minutes is the average time, demonstrated by careful observation, during which strangers in a social situation interact before they decide to part or continue their encounter' (Zunin & Zunin, 1972, p. 6). The outcome of those first few minutes depends on how each person evaluates the other person. Part of the evaluation is based on nonverbal communication. Some of the evaluations involve prediction about personal traits; other evaluations involve predictions about possible behavior. As an exercise in nonverbal communication, please circle the appropriate number to indicate your evaluation of the person in the attached photograph."

Likewise, a mean will be computed for each behavior for each group of participants (i.e., a mean for the group viewing an alcohol T-shirt and a mean for the group viewing a plain T-shirt). These means, along with the results of ANOVA (i.e., F test), will be presented in a table such as Table 2 below.

Table 2
Results for Behaviors Based on Alcohol T-Shirt versus Plain T-Shirt

Trait	Mean for alcohol T-shirt	Mean for plain T-shirt	F	p
Be on time				
Smoke				
Do well in school				
Drink alcohol				
Be a risk taker				
Be violent				
Use illegal drugs				
Be a loser				
Member of "in" crowd				
Party animal				
Get drunk				
Be a sports fan				
Be a good friend				
Use profanity				

Note. Mean scores based on a 7-point scale (7 = *likely* and 1 = *not likely*)

Also, a mean will be computed for all male participants regardless of the type of T-shirt worn; a similar mean will be computed for all female participants. These means, along with the results of ANOVA (i.e., F test), will be presented in a table such as Table 3 below. A corresponding table such as Table 4 on the next page will be constructed for the behaviors.

Table 3
Results for Personal Traits Based on Gender of Adolescent

Trait	Mean for males	Mean for females	F	p
Healthy				
Athletic				
Trustworthy				
Sociable				
Fashionable				
Feminine				
Independent				
Masculine				
Relaxed				
Responsible				
Honest				
Attractive				
Reliable				
Religious				

Note. Mean scores based on a 7-point bipolar scale (7 = *healthy* and 1 = *not healthy*)

Table 4
Results for Behaviors Based on Gender of Adolescent

Trait	Mean for males	Mean for females	F	p
Be on time				
Smoke				
Do well in school				
Drink alcohol				
Be a risk taker				
Be violent				
Use illegal drugs				
Be a loser				
Member of "in" crowd				
Party animal				
Get drunk				
Be a sports fan				
Be a good friend				
Use profanity				

Note. Mean scores based on a 7-point scale (7 = *likely* and 1 = *not likely*)

Implications

Theoretical Implications

The stages of impression formation as proposed by Livesley and Bromley's (1973) theory will be used as the framework for investigating impressions of an adolescent wearing an alcohol promotional T-shirt. The theory predicts that selection of cues leads to formation of impressions of general traits followed by extended inferences. Results of this study will test this aspect of the theory.

Practical Implications

Athletes are linked to sports participation via clothing symbols such as uniforms and letter jackets. Cheerleaders are linked to cheerleading via the clothing symbol of cheerleading uniforms. Likewise, it could be argued that being viewed as a party animal or a risk taker may be linked to such clothing symbols as alcohol promotional T-shirts. Adolescents in Barnett and Miller's (2001) study reported personal norms as one reason for not using alcohol—for example, they were not the kind of person who drinks, that others knew not to offer them alcohol, and that they did not act like they wanted to drink. A decision to wear an alcohol promotional T-shirt might reflect the wearer's personal norms in favor of using alcohol, such as, "I am the kind of person who drinks alcohol," "I would welcome the offer of a drink," or "I want to drink." The results of this study will provide information on other students' reactions to wearing alcohol promotional T-shirts.

Policy Implications

Results of this study may have implications for dress code policies in public schools. Students send messages and advertise alcohol to their peers by wearing alcohol promotional T-shirts. Peer endorsement of alcohol use is likely to be a powerful influence on students who are concerned with conforming to peer norms. School administrators sometimes need empirical evidence to justify a ban on certain clothing items. This study might provide empirical evidence to justify a ban on alcohol promotional clothing items.

According to Starek (1997), "direct or circumstantial evidence of an intent to target children with advertising for a product they cannot legally consume" is relevant to the unfairness issue that "requires showing that advertising causes or is likely to cause substantial injury" (pp. 5–6). Starek noted that there is an absence of reliable scientific evidence concerning the effect of alcohol advertising on consumption of alcohol. The current study will provide an important piece of evidence regarding perceptions associated with alcohol promotional T-shirts and will offer a possible explanation for the appeal of alcohol promotional items based on a hypothesized link between developmental tasks, adolescent norms, and alcohol use. This evidence could be combined with other studies to help build a case for banning the use of T-shirts and other items for promotion of alcohol.

References

Anderson, E., Bell, N., Fischer, J., Munsch, J., Peek, C., & Sorell, G. (1993). Applying a risk-taking perspective. In N. Bell & R. Bell (Eds.), *Adolescent risk taking* (pp. 165–185). Newbury Park, CA: Sage.

Andsager, J., Austin, E., & Pinkleton, B. (2002). Gender as a variable in interpretation of alcohol-related messages. *Communication Research, 29,* 246–270.

Barnett, J., & Miller, M. (2001). Adolescents' reported motivations to use or not to use alcohol or other drugs. *The Social Studies, 92,* 209–212.

Baumrind, D. (1987). A developmental perspective on risk taking in contemporary America. In C. E. Irwin Jr. (Ed.), *Adolescent social behavior and health: New directions for child development* (No. 37, pp. 93–125). San Francisco: Jossey-Bass.

Bell, N., & Bell, R. (1993). *Adolescent risk taking.* Newbury Park, CA: Sage.

Brown, T., Parks, K., Zimmerman, R., & Phillips, C. (2001). The role of religion in predicting adolescent alcohol use and problem drinking. *Journal of Studies on Alcohol, 62,* 696–705.

Covell, K. (1992). The appeal of image advertisements: Age, gender, and product differences. *Journal of Early Adolescence, 12,* 46–60.

Covell, K., Dion, K., & Dion, K. (1994). Gender differences in evaluations of tobacco and alcohol advertisements. *Canadian Journal of Behavioral Sciences, 26,* 404–420.

Darden, D., & Worden, S. (1991). Identity announcement in mass society: The T-shirt. *Sociological Spectrum, 11,* 67–79.

Domzal, T., & Kernan, J. (1992). Reading advertising: The what and how of product meaning. *The Journal of Consumer Marketing, 9,* 48–64.

Du-ude! Clothiers catalog sells students on drinking. (1998, July 24). *Wall Street Journal,* p. B1.

Eicher, J., Baizerman, S., & Michelman, J. (1991). Adolescent dress, part II: A qualitative study of suburban high school students. *Adolescence, 26,* 679–686.

Erikson, E. (1963). *Childhood and society.* New York: Norton.

Erikson, E. (1982). *The life cycle completed: A review.* New York: Norton.

Erikson, E. (1997). *The life cycle completed.* New York: Norton.

Fox, R., Krugman, D., Fletcher, J., & Fischer, P. (1998). Adolescents' attention to beer and cigarette print ads and associated product warnings. *Journal of Advertising, 27,* 57–68.

Gardner, W. (1993). A life-span rational-choice theory of risk taking. In N. Bell & R. Bell (Eds.), *Adolescent risk taking* (pp. 66–83). Newbury Park, CA: Sage.

Gillmore, M., Wells, E., Simpson, E., Morrison, D., Hoppe, M., & Wilsdon, A. (1998). Children's beliefs about drinking. *American Journal of Drug and Alcohol Abuse, 24,* 131–152.

Hanson, D., & Engs, R. (1992). College students' drinking problems: A national study. *Psychological Reports, 71,* 39–42.

Havighurst, R. (1953). *Developmental tasks and education.* New York: Longman.

Irwin, C. (1993). Adolescence and risk taking: How are they related? In N. Bell & R. Bell (Eds.), *Adolescent risk taking* (pp. 7–28). Newbury Park, CA: Sage.

Jeynes, W. (2001). Religious commitment and adolescent behavior. *Journal of Interdisciplinary Studies, 13,* 31–50.

Johnston, L., O'Malley, P., & Bachman, J. (1987). *National trends in drug use and related factors among American high school students and young adults, 1975–1986.* Bethesda, MD: National Institute on Drug Abuse.

Kaiser, S. (1997). *The social psychology of clothing: Symbolic appearances in context.* New York: Fairchild.

Kelly, K., & Edwards, R. (1998). Image advertisements for alcohol products: Is their appeal associated with adolescents' intention to consume alcohol? *Adolescence, 33,* 47–59.

Klaczynski, P. (1990). Cultural-developmental tasks and adolescent development: Theoretical and methodological considerations. *Adolescence, 25,* 811–823.

Komro, K., & Toomey, T. (2002). Strategies to prevent underage drinking. *Alcohol Research & Health, 26,* 5–14.

Kotulak, R. (2002, December 10). American Medical Association calls on television to curtail alcohol ads. *Chicago Tribune,* p. W2.

Kropp, F., Lavack, A., & Holden, S. (1999). Smokers and beer drinkers: Values and consumer susceptibility to interpersonal influence. *Journal of Consumer Marketing, 16*, 536–557.

Kuther, T., & Higgins-D'Alessandro, A. (2000). Bridging the gap between moral reasoning and adolescent engagement in risky behavior. *Journal of Adolescence, 23*, 409–422.

Livesley, W., & Bromley, D. (1973). *Person perception in childhood and adolescence.* New York: John Wiley.

Lyng, S. (1990). Edgework: A social psychological analysis of voluntary risk taking. *American Journal of Sociology, 95*, 851–856.

MacGillivray, M., & Wilson, P. (1997). Clothing and appearance among early, middle, and late adolescents. *Clothing and Textiles Research Journal, 15*, 43–49.

Madden, P., & Grube, J. (1994). The frequency and nature of alcohol and tobacco advertising in televised sports, 1990 through 1992. *American Journal of Public Health, 84*, 297–299.

Martino, W. (1999). "Cool boys," "party animals," "squids" and "poofters": Interrogating the dynamics and politics of adolescent masculinities in school. *British Journal of Sociology of Education, 20*, 239–263.

Mason, A., & Windle, M. (2001). Family, religious, school and peer influences on adolescent alcohol use: A longitudinal study. *Journal of Studies on Alcohol, 62*, 44–53.

Mathios, A., Avery, R., Bisogni, C., & Shanahan, J. (1998). Alcohol portrayal on prime-time television: Manifest and latent messages. *Journal of Studies on Alcohol, 59*, 305–310.

Miller, L., Davies, M., & Greenwald, S. (2000). Religiosity and substance use among adolescents in the National Comorbidity Survey. *Journal of the American Academy of Child and Adolescent Psychiatry, 39*, 1190–1197.

Mitchell, E. (1989, October 16). Same pooch, new pitch. *Time, 134*, 95.

Mosher, J. (1994). Alcohol advertising and public health: An urgent call for action. *American Journal of Public Health, 84*, 180–181.

Newman, B., & Newman, P. (1987). *Development through life: A psychosocial approach.* Chicago: Dorsey.

O'Neal, G. (1998, August). Adolescent dress and risk taking. *Family Science Review, 11*, 190–204.

Parker, B. (1998). Exploring life themes and myths in alcohol advertisements through a meaning-based model of advertising experiences. *The Journal of Advertising,* Spring, 97–112.

Peretti-Watel, P., Beck, F., & Legleye, S. (2002). Beyond the U-curve: The relationship between sports and alcohol, cigarette and cannabis use in adolescents. *Addiction, 97*, 707–716.

Researchers find health problems among teen drinkers. (2001). *The Brown University Digest of Addiction Theory & Application, 20*, 7.

Robert Wood Johnson Foundation. (2001). *Substance abuse: The nation's number one health problem.* Princeton, NJ: Brandeis University.

Santor, D., Messervey, D., & Kusumakar, V. (2000). Measuring peer pressure, popularity, and conformity in adolescent boys and girls: Predicting school performance, sexual attitudes, and substance abuse. *Journal of Youth and Adolescence, 29*, 163–182.

Silbereisen, R., Eyferth, K., & Rudinger, G. (1986). *Development as action in context.* New York: Springer.

Simons-Morton, B., Haynie, D., Crump, A., Saylor, K., Eitel, P., & Yu, K. (1999). Expectancies and other psychosocial factors associated with alcohol use among early adolescent boys and girls. *Addictive Behaviors, 24*, 229–238.

Starek, R. (1997, July 25). *The ABCs at the FTC: Marketing and advertising to children.* Retrieved January 22, 2003, from http://www.ftc.gov/speeches/starek/minnfin.htm.

Stone, G. (1981). Appearance. In G. Stone & H. Farberman (Eds.), *Social psychology through symbolic interaction* (2nd ed., pp. 101–113). New York: John Wiley.

Strasburger, V. (1995). *Adolescents and the media: Medical and psychological impact.* Thousand Oaks, CA: Sage.

Suitor, J., & Carter, R. (1999). Jocks, nerds, babes, and thugs: A research note on regional differences in adolescent gender norms. *Gender Issues, 17*, 87–101.

Suitor, J., Minyard, S., & Carter, R. (2001). "Did you see what I saw?" Gender differences in perceptions of avenues to prestige among adolescents. *Sociological Inquiry, 71*, 437–454.

Suitor, J., & Reavis, R. (1995). Football, fast cars, and cheerleading: Adolescent gender norms, 1978–1989. *Adolescence, 30*, 265–268.

Thorlindsson, T. (2001). Risk behaviour, drug use and sport participation among Icelandic youth. In D. Billet (Ed.), *Sports played by young people and dangerous behaviour* (pp. 64–69). Paris: Ministere de la Jeunesse et des Sports.

Traux, S. (1990, October). To drink? *Current Health, 17*, 12–13.

Treise, D., Wolburg, J., & Otnes, C. (1999). Understanding the "social gifts" of drinking rituals: An alternative framework for PSA developers. *Journal of Advertising, 28*, 17–31.

Urberg, K., Degirmencioglu, S., & Pilgrim, C. (1997). Close friend and group influence on adolescent cigarette smoking and alcohol use. *Developmental Psychology, 33*, 834–844.

Waiters, E., Treno, A., & Grube, J. (2001). Alcohol advertising and youth: A focus-group analysis of what young people find appealing in alcohol advertising. *Contemporary Drug Problems, 28*, 695–718.

Wallack, L., Grube, J., Madden, P., & Breed, W. (1990). Portrayals of alcohol on prime-time television. *Journal of Studies on Alcohol, 51*, 428–437.

Workman, J., & Johnson, K. (1994). Effects of conformity and nonconformity to gender-role expectations for dress: Teachers versus students. *Adolescence, 29,* 207–223.

Zunin, L., & Zunin, N. (1972). *Contact: The first four minutes.* New York: Ballantine Books.

Notes

Model Proposal 7: Qualitative Research with Focus Groups

Effective Strategies for Esteem-Enhancement: What Do Young Adolescents Have to Say?[1]

A Research Proposal Based on the Work of

David L. DuBois

Kelle Reach

Erika M. Lockerd

Gilbert R. Parra

Beginning with the affective education movement of the 1960s, the past several decades have witnessed a remarkable proliferation of programs to enhance the self-esteem of youth (Du-Bois & Tevendale, 1999; Harter, 1999; Hattie, 1992). Self-esteem has been defined as the "evaluation which an individual makes and customarily maintains with regard to himself [or herself]" (Rosenberg, 1965, p. 5). Theorists have emphasized the affective nature of the construct and frequently used terms such as *feelings of self-worth* and *positive self-regard* to refer to the subjective experience of self-esteem (Harter, 1999). Self-esteem has been distinguished on this basis from other self-system constructs such as self-concept, although the practical importance of these distinctions is not yet clearly established (Byrne, 1996).

Currently, there is a recognized need for efforts that specifically target the period of transition from childhood to adolescence. It is during early adolescence that the search for a coherent identity intensifies. It thus is a stage of development that represents a critical window of opportunity to cultivate a strong sense of self-worth in the emerging personality (Brinthaupt & Lipka, 2002). Young adolescents, however, frequently experience difficulty maintaining positive self-esteem in the wake of the myriad areas of stress and change that characterize the transition. As many as 1 in 5 youth report high levels of self-esteem in late childhood, only to exhibit a progressive and substantial decline in feelings of self-worth during early adolescence (DuBois & Tevendale, 1999). Negative self-esteem trajectories experienced by young adolescents in turn are predictive of significant difficulties in emotional, behavioral, and academic functioning (Silverthorn & Crombie, 2002).

The aim of strengthening self-esteem during early adolescence is consistent with the goals of recent large-scale initiatives to promote positive youth development (America's Promise: The Alliance for Youth, 1999; Carnegie Council on Adolescent Development, 1995; National Research Council [NRC], 2002). Indeed, as a core component of positive mental health (Durlak, 2000), self-esteem has been an appealing focus for a range of promotive and preventive interventions. Strategies to enhance self-esteem, however, have demonstrated only limited effectiveness and are in need of refinement and innovation (Haney & Durlak, 1998). Self-esteem is understood to have a complex, multidimensional structure, for example, and to be shaped by experiences in multiple areas (Kernis, 2002). Accordingly, general feelings of self-worth alone are not a reliable predictor of positive adjustment (Harter, 1998). Findings are strong only when also considering

---

[1] This proposal was adapted from a report of completed research by DuBois, D. L., Lockerd, E. M., Reach, K., & Parra, G. R. (2003). Effective strategies for esteem-enhancement: What do young adolescents have to say? *Journal of Early Adolescence, 23*, 405–434. Copyright © 2003 by Sage Publications, Inc. Reprinted with permission. Correspondence about the completed research may be addressed to David L. DuBois, Community Health Sciences, School of Public Health (MC 923), University of Illinois at Chicago, Chicago, IL 60612-4324. Electronic mail may be sent to dldubois@uic.edu. The affiliations of the authors are: David L. DuBois, University of Illinois at Chicago; and Erika M. Lockerd, Kelle Reach, and Gilbert R. Parra, University of Missouri–Columbia.

more specific aspects or sources of self-esteem, such as those based on experiences in the family, school, and peer group (Harter, 1998). Most self-esteem programs, however, have focused on promoting feelings of worth in an undifferentiated manner (DuBois, Burk-Braxton, & Tevendale, 2002). Many programs, furthermore, have relied exclusively on the use of structured curricula and thus have not incorporated the environmental changes or supports necessary to strengthen self-esteem in key areas of participants' lives (DuBois et al., 2002). Neither has adequate attention been devoted to the need for approaches that promote *healthy* self-esteem (Harter, 1999). Without strategies to ensure that feelings of worth have an adaptive and realistic basis, interventions may be of limited or no value in facilitating desired outcomes (e.g., academic achievement). When high levels of self-esteem are derived in ways that lack a healthy foundation, they also can contribute to youth engaging in negative behaviors (e.g., drinking and aggression) (Salmivalli, 2001; Scheier, Botvin, Griffin, & Diaz, 2000). Motivation to feel good about oneself is assumed to be nearly universal and to exert a profound influence on behavior (Harter, 1999). Therefore, strategies that ensure youth fulfill that need in a healthy manner are essential.

Focus groups are one widely recommended approach to informing the design of more effective interventions (Bartholomew, Parcel, & Kok, 1998; Institute of Medicine [IOM], 1994; Morgan, 1997). Focus groups offer a means of obtaining valuable input from representatives of the target population regarding both the problem to be addressed (e.g., sources of low self-esteem) and viable change strategies (e.g., methods of esteem-enhancement). Such information then can be used to design programs tailored to the needs and preferences of the ultimate "consumers" (e.g., young adolescents), thereby increasing likely levels of participation and the potential for positive outcomes (Bartholomew et al., 1998). In the proposed research, focus groups will be conducted with young adolescents to help inform the development of beneficial esteem-enhancement strategies for their age group.

Effectiveness of Existing Esteem-Enhancement Programs

Two literature reviews have considered the effectiveness of esteem-enhancement programs using meta-analysis (Haney & Durlak, 1998; Hattie, 1992). Hattie (1992) reported an average effect size of .37 for 89 program evaluations. Haney and Durlak (1998) found a similar average effect size of .27 based on evaluations of 120 programs. Of those programs, 107 included participants in the age range of early adolescence (i.e., between the ages of 10 and 15 years old).[2] Youth in self-esteem programs also exhibited positive change in the areas of behavior, personality/emotional functioning, and academic performance. Programs that produced the largest effects on such outcomes, furthermore, were those in which participants experienced the greatest increases in self-concept or self-esteem (Haney & Durlak, 1998).

There are several important qualifications, however, to the preceding findings. First, results indicate that gains for program participants in self-esteem and other areas of adjustment were only small to moderate in magnitude (Haney & Durlak, 1998). Furthermore, such estimates are likely to be inflated because only a small proportion of esteem-enhancement programs have been evaluated formally and those that have seem to be among the most well designed (Hattie, 1992). Second, interventions have had only limited success in producing improvements in self-esteem that are sustained over time (Haney & Durlak, 1998; Hattie, 1992). Some positive effects, for example, appear to be attributable to euphoria or good feelings at the end of programs that dissipate relatively quickly thereafter (Marsh, Richards, & Barnes, 1986).

A third concern is that esteem-enhancement programs targeting young adolescents have not been as effective as those involving other age groups (DuBois et al., 2002). Hattie (1992), for example, reported higher average effect sizes for programs with adults (.52) and children (.31) in comparison to those in which participants were preadolescents (.20) or adolescents (.23). Trends

---

[2] The number of programs that included youth in the age range of early adolescence was determined on the basis of a review of source articles for the Haney and Durlak (1998) meta-analysis, conducted by authors of the present study.

toward less effectiveness during early adolescence likely are a reflection in part of the unique characteristics of the age group. Efforts to work with young adolescents are complicated by their rapid and varying rates of growth in all areas of development, including those that have a direct bearing on self-esteem (e.g., identity) (Lerner, 1988). Young adolescents also do not have as a group the cognitive abilities required to respond well to the didactic approaches used in many programs (Harter, 1999). Several considerations thus make it a challenging proposition to design effective esteem-enhancement strategies for young adolescents (Brinthaupt & Lipka, 2002).

A final concern is that programs have not been equally effective in strengthening the self-esteem of all youth. They have had their greatest effects on those who enter programs already exhibiting low self-esteem or difficulties in other areas (Haney & Durlak, 1998; Hattie, 1992). In comparison, only modest benefits are apparent for less vulnerable or at-risk youth.[3] Existing strategies, therefore, would not be effective necessarily for preventing declines in self-esteem (and onset of adjustment problems) for those youth who enter early adolescence exhibiting relatively healthy functioning (DuBois et al., 2002).

Need for a Youth Perspective

Several promising directions for addressing limitations of existing approaches to esteem-enhancement have been proposed in the theoretical and empirical literature (Beane, 1994; DuBois & Tevendale, 1999; Gurney, 1987; Hamachek, 1994; Haney & Durlak, 1998; Harter, 1999; Hattie, 1992). Based on a review of those considerations, DuBois and colleagues (2002) recently discussed several recommendations for intervention strategies to strengthen self-esteem during early adolescence. It was noted, however, that apparently no attention had been devoted to obtaining the perspective of young adolescents themselves on the content or design of interventions (DuBois et al., 2002).

The failure to systematically incorporate young adolescents' input into program planning is a noteworthy omission for several reasons. First, as qualitative data that reflect experientially derived knowledge (Patton, 1990), the views of young adolescents may highlight promising directions for the design of more effective esteem-enhancement strategies. Second, giving young adolescents direct voice in the design of interventions has the potential to increase their levels of participation and positive engagement in resulting programs (Zeldin, McDaniel, Topitzes, & Calvert, 2000). Programs that can be advertised as developed in such a "consumer-friendly" manner are likely to be viewed by young adolescents as more credible, thus facilitating greater levels of involvement (Morgan, 1997). Finally, obtaining input directly from young adolescents provides a mechanism for helping to ensure that the needs and preferences of members of their age group with diverse characteristics and backgrounds are addressed in programs. Currently, data on program effectiveness are lacking for several demographic subgroups (e.g., low-income and minority), thus underscoring a need to learn more about the views and experiences of young adolescents from varied backgrounds (DuBois et al., 2002).

Proposed Study

The focus groups in the present research are designed to address each of the preceding areas of concern. For insight into the experiential knowledge of young adolescents, participants will be asked to share their views regarding factors that influence the self-esteem of those in their age group as well as views about possible sources of unhealthy self-esteem among their peers. In an effort to ensure sensitivity to the voices of young adolescents as consumers of interventions, par-

---

[3] Another possible factor contributing to weaker effects for programs that include youth who begin with relatively high self-esteem is ceiling effects on outcome measures. During early adolescence, however, substantial numbers of youth with high levels of self-esteem can be expected to exhibit declines on measures in the absence of intervention (Silverthorn & Crombie, 2002). If programs were effective in preventing such declines, they thus could have large effects even on those who enter with high self-esteem (DuBois, Burk-Braxton, & Tevendale, 2002).

ticipants will be given the opportunity to design their own hypothetical, ideal esteem-enhancement programs. They also will be asked to discuss factors that affect their levels of enjoyment of and engagement in adult-organized activities or programs more generally. Finally, the need for input from a diverse group of young adolescents will be addressed by the selection of participants with varying demographic characteristics (e.g., low-income family background) as well as varying levels of self-esteem.

Method

Sample

Participants will be approximately 60 young adolescents attending a sixth- and seventh-grade public middle school in a medium-sized Midwestern city. They will be selected from a larger group of 508 students within the school's general population who recently participated in a survey-based research project (for details, see Lopez & DuBois, 2001). A stratified random selection process will be used to identify those from the larger pool of students who will be asked to participate in the present study. In an effort to facilitate comfortable and productive group discussions (Morgan & Krueger, 1998), young adolescents for each focus group will be selected for similarity on one of the following characteristics: level of self-esteem (low or relatively high), gender, race/ethnicity (white or African American), grade level (sixth or seventh), or family socioeconomic status (SES) (low or not low). Because there are two possible categories for each of the five selection factors, a total of 10 groups are planned (i.e., one group for those with low self-esteem, another comprised of all those with relatively high esteem, another all males, etc.). Levels of self-esteem will be distinguished as low or relatively high based on a cutoff score for the Global Self-Esteem Scale of the Self-Esteem Questionnaire (SEQ) (DuBois, Felner, Brand, Phillips, & Lease, 1996), a measure completed in the larger research project. To facilitate identification of potential participants with low self-esteem, the cutoff score that will be used (i.e., 20) is approximately one standard deviation below the mean for the overall sample ($M = 25.09$, $SD = 4.68$). Family socioeconomic status will be categorized as low if the student in the larger research project reported participating in the school's subsidized lunch program or indicated family financial limitations on one other pertinent survey item.

Through use of the preceding criteria, students who qualify for each of the 10 planned focus groups will be identified. From each of these sets of students, 9 will be selected randomly for participation in the relevant group, thus resulting in a total of 90 potential participants in the research. Participation will require parent consent and young adolescent assent. Group size will range from 4 to 8 participants.

The following demographics of the final sample will be compared with those of the student population of the participating school: (1) gender, (2) race/ethnicity, and (3) socioeconomic status. Chi-square analysis will determine if the final sample is significantly different from the school population, providing an indication of the extent to which the sample is representative of the larger population from which it will be selected.

Procedure

Each focus group will meet for 2 hours in a comfortable room on a university campus. Following recommended procedure (Morgan & Krueger, 1998), each group will be led by a moderator and an assistant moderator. Moderators will include the first author (a licensed child clinical psychologist), who will moderate three groups, and study co-authors (doctoral students in clinical psychology), who will moderate all remaining groups. Assistant moderators will include study co-authors as well as trained undergraduate research assistants. Moderators and assistant moderators will receive an average of 25 hours of training from a doctoral-level psychologist (first author of the current study) experienced in conducting focus groups. Training will include assigned readings, didactic instruction, role playing, and supervised participation in one to two pilot focus groups with youth.

With permission of participants and their parents, all focus group discussions will be audiorecorded. The audiotape for each focus group will be transcribed in its entirety. All written materials (e.g., participant worksheets) will also be transcribed into the same word processing file.

Focus Group Protocol

The focus group protocol will follow the moderately structured group format (Morgan & Krueger, 1998), which uses prewritten questions and activities but allows for deviations when appropriate. A summary of focus group questions and activities is provided in the Appendix near the end of this proposal.[4] As shown in the Appendix, initial questions (i.e., 1 and 2) ask participants for general input on factors likely to affect their motivation to participate in activities or programs organized by adults. The next questions (i.e., 3 and 4) ask about positive and negative sources of influence on self-esteem during early adolescence. Self-esteem is defined for participants as feeling good about oneself as a person (Harter, 1999). Following open-ended discussions for each of those questions, group members will individually complete a brief worksheet in which they will be asked to write down any additional ideas on the topics. The worksheet will provide an opportunity for less vocal group members to share their views in an alternative format. It also will serve as a reflective activity to help stimulate further input from all participants (Morgan & Krueger, 1998). For this reason, completion of worksheets will be followed by another period of group discussion. Toward the end of the discussion, the group will be asked about the personal characteristic or background factor shared by members of the group (e.g., being female) and its relevance to self-esteem at their age (i.e., Question 5). In several instances (e.g., gender, race/ethnicity, and grade level), the factor that group members have in common will be self-evident. In other instances (e.g., level of self-esteem and family socioeconomic status), for reasons of sensitivity and respect for privacy, the question will be posed in a way that does not overtly reference the fact that all group members share the characteristic involved (e.g., low self-esteem). Finally, the first half of each focus group will conclude with a discussion of participants' observations regarding possible unhealthy sources of self-esteem among their age group (i.e., Question 6).

The latter half of each focus group session will consist of activities designed to elicit participant input on effective strategies for esteem-enhancement. Working in small groups (i.e., 2 or 3 persons), participants first will be asked to create a story about a hypothetical young adolescent with low self-esteem (i.e., Question 7). They will then be asked to design a program that would be effective in promoting healthy self-esteem for the same young adolescent (i.e., Question 8). The moderator, assistant moderator, and additional trained research assistants will circulate among the small groups to facilitate the work of participants while taking care not to dictate the content of their ideas. In an effort to provide some minimal degree of structure for the program design activity, each small group will be given a large sheet to work on that will include *who*, *when*, *where*, and *what* prompts. Following each activity (i.e., story creation and program design), participants will take turns presenting their work to the rest of the group. In doing so, the moderator will have participants elaborate on important themes or ideas.

It is felt that the term *program* used in different portions of the focus group protocol will be more easily understood by youth than an alternative term such as *intervention*. The term *program* is intended to connote a psychosocial intervention rather than an isolated activity or event. This view will be emphasized to youth by focus group moderators and research assistants.

---

[4] A detailed version of the focus group protocol and related materials (e.g., worksheets) will be developed and reviewed prior to conducting the study.

Data Coding and Analysis

Data coding and analysis will occur in several phases. First, based on careful review of focus group transcripts by the study authors, several general categories of content will be distinguished. The purpose in doing so is to provide a broad structure within which to carry out more refined data coding and analysis activities (Morgan & Krueger, 1998). At the most general level, a distinction will be made between material that emphasizes naturally occurring influences on early adolescent self-esteem and that which addresses strategies for intervention. Within naturally occurring influences, further differentiation will be made in three areas: (a) whether individual or environmental factors affecting self-esteem were being discussed, (b) what (if any) life domain(s) were involved (e.g., peers, school, etc.), and (c) what (if any) personal or background characteristics were implicated (e.g., gender, race/ethnicity, etc.). In addition, three differing directions or patterns of influence on self-esteem (as perceived by participants) will be distinguished: healthy raising of self-esteem, lowering of self-esteem, and unhealthy raising of self-esteem. With respect to strategies for intervention, separate categories will be established corresponding to the *who*, *when*, *where*, and *what* prompts used in the program design exercise. An additional category will be created for factors discussed by participants as affecting their levels of enjoyment and engagement generally in programs or activities organized by adults (i.e., "enjoyability").

The second phase will involve detailed coding of individual statements (oral as well as written) made by participants during each focus group. Statements will be considered to be expressions of distinct ideas. As such, individual statements generally correspond to a given participant's turn speaking in a discussion. In some instances, multiple statements will be distinguished within a relatively lengthy single comment, or, alternatively, a short series of comments together by the same participant will be counted as only one statement.

Coders will be study authors and trained undergraduate assistants. Interrater reliability will be assessed through random selection of 200 statements (20 statements from each focus group), which will then be coded by study authors a second time (excluding any they originally coded themselves). Percentage interrater agreement will be calculated.

The third phase of data coding and analysis will involve combining similar codes into larger groupings or categories using the affinity process (Brassard, 1989). The affinity procedure is a variant of the Q-sort process and has been used in previous focus group research with adolescents (Lindsey & Kalafat, 1998). Briefly, the process involves having several persons work together to place items into categories that each share a common theme. After consensus is reached, similar groupings are joined together and arranged hierarchically in a diagram (see Brassard, 1989, for further details). For present purposes, separate affinity diagrams will be derived for codes assigned within each of the following general categories: individual or environmental influences on self-esteem, influences on self-esteem pertaining to differing life domains (e.g., peers), and intervention strategies (i.e., who, when, where, what, and enjoyment of programs).[5] To guard against unintended loss of information through the affinity process, the research team will be divided into two groups that will work independently to derive separate diagrams for each set of codes. Discrepancies will be reconciled by study authors through discussion.

A further aspect of the affinity process involves combining differing sets of diagrams into summary diagrams for purposes of parsimony and avoiding redundancy in findings. Separate summary diagrams will be derived for naturally occurring influences on self-esteem and intervention strategies. The entire research team will be involved in the process, led by the study authors. As a final step, determinations of intensity and direction of influence on self-esteem will be made for each relevant theme in the summary diagrams. Intensity designations will be based primarily on the number of statements coded as relevant to each theme. In cases in which more than one

---

[5] Categories of codes pertaining to personal or background characteristics of young adolescents (e.g., gender) will not be subjected to the affinity process because of their anticipated relatively small number; however, they will be included in the summary diagram for naturally occurring influences on self-esteem.

participant is credited with making or endorsing a statement (e.g., group agreement with a comment), statements will be weighted by the relevant number of participants to more accurately reflect their relative prevalence. Based on inspection of the distribution of overall frequency of statements made relevant to differing themes, cut-points will be selected to help guide intensity designations of high (H), moderate (M), or low (L). Designations of primary perceived direction of influence on self-esteem will be derived in a similar manner (i.e., inspection of frequency distributions for relevant codes) but will be made only for themes pertaining to naturally occurring influences on self-esteem (intervention strategies by definition will be intended to raise self-esteem). Designations will include: healthy raising (+), lowering (–), raising/lowering (+/– [i.e., a relatively equal mixture of the preceding two designations]), and unhealthy raising (U).

Discussion of Limitations and Future Directions

Several limitations and directions for future research should be noted. As in most qualitative research (Patton, 1990), the relatively small size of the sample will potentially limit generalizability of findings. Participants with varying demographic backgrounds and levels of self-esteem will be selected purposefully to give voice to a cross-section of young adolescents. The resulting sample, however, will not be random and thus cannot be assumed to be representative of members of the targeted groups. It also would be valuable in the future to obtain input from a wider range of young adolescents, including those from other minority groups (e.g., Hispanic) and geographic settings (e.g., inner city). The views of other important constituencies for esteem-enhancement interventions (e.g., parents) should receive consideration as well.

Participants' recommendations for intervention that will be derived from this study must be qualified for several reasons. Participants will be instructed to design a program for young adolescents with low self-esteem. It is possible, however, that some recommendations will be general and not intended to be specific to improving self-esteem. In addition, some participants in the research might not be able to distinguish between activities and programs they simply would find enjoyable and those expected to actually result in beneficial outcomes.

Finally, all of the areas of program innovation suggested by participant input in this proposed study will later require formal testing and evaluation. Ideally, the suggestions should be incorporated into future interventions and then examined with respect to their ability to strengthen outcomes relative to more traditional esteem-enhancement procedures (IOM, 1994). There is evidence, moreover, of positive outcomes associated with infusion of youth involvement throughout all stages of decision making, planning, and implementation in community-based programs (Zeldin et al., 2000). One strategy for ensuring such infusion would be to establish a permanent advisory council of young adolescents with diverse backgrounds and experiences (IOM, 1994). Integration of mechanisms for input from young adolescents into programs themselves is a logical extension of the proposed study and could be of significant value in strengthening the effectiveness of esteem-enhancement interventions during early adolescence.

Appendix

Summary of Focus Group Questions and Activities

1. We're going to be organizing some activities for kids your age. Besides learning something, we want them to have a good time and be interested in coming back. What makes an activity or program organized by adults fun in this way?

2. Now let's talk about the opposite question. What things make an activity or program a turn-off? That is, what types of things make it boring, uncomfortable, or something you don't want to do again?

3. Let's talk about *self-esteem*. What helps persons your age to have *high* self-esteem, to feel good about who they are as a person?

4. What kinds of things make it *difficult* for persons your age to have high self-esteem—that is, what makes them feel less good about themselves or have *low* self-esteem? [Participants will complete individual worksheets asking for additional ideas and opinions about factors influencing self-esteem during early adolescence.]

5. Is there anything about [personal characteristic shared by group members—e.g., being male] that makes it easier or harder to feel good about yourself at your age?

6. Does anyone think there are times when persons your age have high self-esteem but it is not *healthy* self-esteem? By healthy, we mean something that is good for them *overall*—that is, their emotional, behavioral, academic, and physical well-being.

7. Now we are going to do an exercise. You are going to make up a story about a month in the life of someone of your age who has *low* self-esteem or at least does by the end of the month—they'll start off with one of these I Am Lovable and Capable, or IALAC, signs and then not have one by the time the month is over. You will work with one or two other group members. Write down the main ideas of your group's story; you can include pictures with it too if you would like. We want to know everything that happens to the person and what they do, think, and feel as they go through the entire month.

8. Next, you are going to make up a story about the same person, but it is in the future and he or she has participated in a self-esteem intervention program. As a result of being in the program, he or she now has high self-esteem; it is also *healthy* self-esteem. We want to know what kind of program helped the person's self-esteem to improve. Think of the program in any way you want—it could last any amount of time you want and have sessions or activities as often as you want; it can happen anywhere and include anyone from the person's life. *This does not have to be like any program you've ever been to or heard about—please just tell us about any ideas you have!*

References

America's Promise: The Alliance for Youth. (1999). *Report to the nation: 1999.* Alexandria, VA: Author.

Bartholomew, L. K., Parcel, G. S., & Kok, G. (1998). Intervention mapping: A process for developing theory- and evidence-based health education programs. *Health Education Behavior, 25,* 545–563.

Beane, J. A. (1994). Cluttered terrain: The schools' interest in the self. In T. M. Brinthaupt & R. P. Lipka (Eds.), *Changing the self: Philosophies, techniques, and experiences* (pp. 69–87). Albany: State University of New York Press.

Brassard, M. (1989). *The memory jogger plus.* Methuen, MA: Goal/QPC.

Brinthaupt, T. M., & Lipka, R. P. (Eds.). (2002). *Understanding early adolescent self and identity: Applications and interventions.* Albany: State University of New York Press.

Byrne, B. M. (1996). *Measuring self-concept across the life span: Issues and instrumentation.* Washington, DC: American Psychological Association.

Carnegie Council on Adolescent Development. (1995). *Great transitions: Preparing adolescents for a new century.* Washington, DC: Carnegie Corporation.

DuBois, D. L., Burk-Braxton, C., & Tevendale, H. D. (2002). Esteem-enhancement interventions during early adolescence. In T. M. Brinthaupt & R. P. Lipka (Eds.), *Understanding early adolescent self and identity: Applications and interventions* (pp. 321–371). Albany: State University of New York Press.

DuBois, D. L., Felner, R. D., Brand, S., Phillips, R. S. C., & Lease, A. M. (1996). Early adolescent self-esteem: A developmental-ecological framework and assessment strategy. *Journal of Research on Adolescence, 6,* 543–579.

DuBois, D. L., & Tevendale, H. D. (1999). Self-esteem in childhood and adolescence: Vaccine or epiphenomenon? *Applied and Preventive Psychology, 8,* 103–117.

Durlak, J. A. (2000). Health promotion as a strategy in primary prevention. In D. Cicchetti, J. Rappaport, I. Sandler, & R. P. Weissberg (Eds.), *The promotion of wellness in children and adolescents* (pp. 221–241). Washington, DC: CWLA Press.

Gurney, P. W. (1987). Self-esteem in the classroom II: Experiments in enhancement. *School Psychology International, 8,* 21–29.

Hamachek, D. (1994). Changes in the self from a developmental/psychosocial perspective. In T. M. Brinthaupt & R. P. Lipka (Eds.), *Changing the self: Philosophies, techniques, and experiences* (pp. 21–68). Albany: State University of New York Press.

Haney, P., & Durlak, J. A. (1998). Changing self-esteem in children and adolescents: A meta-analytic review. *Journal of Clinical Child Psychology, 27*, 423–433.

Harter, S. (1998). The development of self-representations. In W. Damon (Series Ed.) & N. Eisenberg (Vol. Ed.), *Handbook of child psychology: Vol. 3. Social, emotional, and personality development* (5th ed., pp. 553–617). New York: John Wiley.

Harter, S. (1999). *The construction of the self: A developmental perspective.* New York: Guilford.

Hattie, J. (1992). *Self-concept.* Hillsdale, NJ: Lawrence Erlbaum.

Henggeler, S. W., Schoenwald, S. K., Borduin, C. M., Rowland, M. D., & Cunningham, P. B. (1998). *Multisystemic treatment of antisocial behavior in children and adolescents.* New York: Guilford.

Institute of Medicine. (1994). *Reducing risks for mental disorders.* Washington, DC: National Academy Press.

Kernis, M. H. (2002). Self-esteem as a multifaceted construct. In T. M. Brinthaupt & R. P. Lipka (Eds.), *Understanding early adolescent self and identity: Applications and interventions* (pp. 57–88). Albany: State University of New York Press.

Lerner, R. M. (1988). Early adolescent transitions: The lore and laws of adolescence. In M. D. Levine & E. R. McAnarney (Eds.), *Early adolescent transitions* (pp. 1–21). Lexington, MA: D. C. Heath.

Lindsey, C. R., & Kalafat, J. (1998). Adolescents' views of preferred helper characteristics and barriers to seeking help from school-based adults. *Journal of Educational and Psychological Consultation, 9*, 171–193.

Lopez, C., & DuBois, D. L. (2001, June). *Positive adaptation and mental health in early adolescence.* Paper presented at Eighth Biennial Conference on Community Research and Action, Atlanta, GA.

Marsh, H. W., Richards, G. E., & Barnes, J. (1986). Multidimensional self-concepts: A long term follow-up of the effect of participation in an Outward Bound program. *Personality and Social Psychology Bulletin, 12*, 475–492.

Morgan, D. L. (1997). *Focus groups as qualitative research* (2nd ed.). Thousand Oaks, CA: Sage.

Morgan, D. L., & Krueger, R. A. (1998). *The focus group kit.* Thousand Oaks, CA: Sage.

National Research Council. (2002). *Community programs to promote youth development.* Washington, DC: National Academy Press.

Patton, M. Q. (1990). *Qualitative evaluation and research methods* (2nd ed.). Newbury Park, CA: Sage.

Rosenberg, M. (1965). *Society and adolescent self-image.* Princeton, NJ: Princeton University.

Salmivalli, C. (2001). Feeling good about oneself, being bad to others? Remarks on self-esteem, hostility, and aggressive behavior. *Aggression & Violent Behavior, 6*, 375–393.

Scheier, L. M., Botvin, G. J., Griffin, K. W., & Diaz, T. (2000). Dynamic growth models of self-esteem and adolescent alcohol use. *Journal of Early Adolescence, 20*, 178–209.

Silverthorn, N., & Crombie, G. (2002, April). Longitudinal examination of self-esteem from grades 8 to 11: Identification and psychosocial differences of four trajectory groups. In D. L. DuBois (Chair), *Change and stability in self-esteem during adolescence: The long and the short of it.* Symposium conducted at the Biennial Meeting of the Society for Research on Adolescence, New Orleans, LA.

Zeldin, S., McDaniel, A. K., Topitzes, D., & Calvert, M. (2000). *Youth in decision-making: A study of the impacts of youth on adults and organizations.* Chevy Chase, MD: National 4-H Council.

Notes

Model Proposal 8: Qualitative Research with Interviews

Feeling the Beat: The Meaning of Rap Music for Ethnically Diverse Midwestern College Students—A Phenomenological Study[1]

A Research Proposal Based on the Work of

Derek K. Iwamoto   John Creswell

Leon Caldwell

ABSTRACT

Despite its national and international appeal, rap is considered one of the most controversial of music genres. Given the political charge it generates, rap music has spawned research across the social and health sciences. The majority of the research has investigated its impact on African Americans. Further, the research has tended to focus on negative aspects of the music; there has been a dearth of in-depth qualitative studies that explore how rap impacts the listener. A phenomenological approach was selected for this study in order to capture the essence of how individuals interpret, process, and experience rap music. Our phenomenological study will explore the impact on ethnically diverse college students. The results may have implications for ways rap music can be utilized with adolescents in fields such as education, risk reduction programs, and counseling psychology.

Over the past two decades, rap music has exploded onto the music scene and become one of the most popular and controversial music genres in America. In 2003, the number-one selling artist, according to Billboard Records, was a former drug dealer and survivor of seven gunshot wounds—rapper 50 Cent. Myriad other rappers shattered the top 50 records sold in 2003, and in 2004 the pattern continued (Billboard Records, 2004). Many rappers, such as PDiddy, Eminem, and Snoop Dogg, are now household names. An example of this was in the 2004 presidential election campaign, when PDiddy used his popularity and clout to increase youth voter turnout.

The popularity of rap is not confined to America. In its exponential growth, it has gained international appeal. In France, rap has become a "social and cultural phenomenon" for adolescents (Miranda & Claes, 2004, p. 113). French-Canadian adolescents report that rap music is their favorite musical preference. Youth in Japan have also embraced rap music and emulate facets of the hip hop culture, such as attire, hairstyles, and vernacular. Despite rap's global popularity, it is still largely seen as deviant music by many: Politicians from both political spectrums, powerful religious organizations, and much of the general public condemn it. Rappers have been vilified and labeled as misogynistic and violent (Sullivan, 2003). Rap fans have been viewed as prone to

---

[1] This proposal was adapted from a report of completed research by Iwamoto, D. K., Creswell, J., & Caldwell, L. (2007). Feeling the beat: The meaning of rap music for ethnically diverse Midwestern college students—A phenomenological study. *Adolescence, 42,* 337–351. Copyright © 2007 by Libra Publishers, Inc. Reprinted with permission. Correspondence about the completed research may be addressed to Derek K. Iwamoto, Division of Prevention and Community Research, Yale University School of Medicine, 389 Whitney Avenue, New Haven, CT 06511. Electronic mail may be sent to derek.iwamoto@gmail.com. The affiliations of the authors are: Derek K. Iwamoto, Yale University School of Medicine; and John Creswell and Leon Caldwell, University of Nebraska–Lincoln.

violence and at risk of engaging in unhealthy behaviors (Rose, 1994). Due to the extreme feelings and opinions elicited by rap, it has caught the attention of social scientists.

There has been burgeoning research on the psychological effects of rap on its listeners, and some negative and positive predictors have been identified as to how this music interacts with certain psychological variables. The 2.5-year longitudinal study by Wingood et al. (2003) of 522 single, lower-socioeconomic-status African American female teenagers found that those who had greater exposure to rap music videos were more likely to engage in unhealthy behaviors, such as acts of violence and using drugs or alcohol, and were more likely to have acquired sexually transmitted diseases than those with less exposure. Wingood et al. concluded that what is depicted in the videos may influence adolescents by modeling these unhealthy behaviors. Rubin, West, and Mitchell's (2001) study found that rap music listeners tended to exhibit higher levels of aggression than did listeners of other music genres, but they also had higher levels of self-esteem and lower levels of trust and faith in others.

Rap as an Educational and Counseling Tool

Some research has pointed to the possible use of rap videos and music as a potentially innovative educational and counseling tool. Watts and Abdul-Adil (2002) consider rap a "powerful hook" that can engage young men to rethink and redefine their conceptions of masculinity. Further, they note their successful educational and youth development program that uses rap music videos with adolescent African American males. The program has participants critically analyze their environment and address such concerns as gender, culture, race, and social class primarily through rap videos and movies. Rap music also has been used in HIV/AIDS-prevention counseling with African American adolescents and young adults (Stephens, Braithwaite, & Taylor, 1998). Stephens et al.'s model uses rap music as a "focal point for self-expression, teaching, and learning" (p. 130). In their four-session group-counseling model, participants listen to selected songs and identify, role play, and discuss the messages and risk behaviors in the music. Stephens et al. (1998) feel that rap music is an effective counseling medium because the music is culturally and sociopolitically relevant to many of the participants and facilitates the cooperative learning process. Tyson's (2002) experimental study examining two group counseling conditions (hip hop vs. control) found that rap music as a primary intervention improved the therapeutic experience and outcome for the youths. This research is promising; however, it is limited because it focused mostly on how hip hop/rap music psychologically affects African Americans but not other ethnic minority groups. This gap is particularly striking because racial differences can affect how other ethnic groups, such as Latinos, might experience hip hop and rap music (Sullivan, 2003). Our phenomenological study will address this gap by exploring how this music is experienced and processed, as well as how it impacts the lives of ethnically diverse college students, including Latinos, Asian Americans, whites, and African Americans.

Definitions and History of Terms

Rap is rooted in the African oral traditions, which include speaking rhythmically, having rhythmic beats, call-and-response patterns, and story telling. Richardson and Scott (2002) define rap music as a form of political commentary of the conditions of lower-income African Americans.

Rap music emerged in New York City during the mid-1970s and gained American mainstream appeal in the early and mid-1980s (Sullivan, 2003). The rap music genre is constantly evolving and has a diversity of styles (e.g., gangsta rap, political/socially conscious rap, dance rap, commercialized rap, as well as regional differences) and genres (old school, late 1980s, and new school, after that period) (Sullivan, 2003).

Hip hop refers to the cultural movement among African American youth that is expressed through certain language, clothing, and way of life. Sullivan (2003) describes the various elements of hip hop culture as "rapping, break dancing, graffiti art, and DJing" (p. 619). The term hip hop also will be used here to describe this musical genre/form and is used in conjunction with rap.

Research Questions

The three broad research questions that will guide this study are: (1) What is the meaning ascribed to rap music by ethnically and racially diverse Midwestern college students? (2) What is the context in which they experience rap music? (3) How can rap music be used to deal with everyday stressors, and how does it alter a person's mood?

Method

A phenomenological approach was selected for this proposed study in order to capture the essence of how individuals interpret, process, and experience rap music. This type of qualitative inquiry is considered a rigorous and thorough scientific method of research (Moerer-Urdahl & Creswell, 2004; Moustakas, 1994). Phenomenology is primarily rooted in the seminal works of the existential philosopher Edmund Husserl, as well as philosophers Rene Descartes and Immanuel Kant. Moustakas (1994) defines phenomenology as "knowledge as it appears to consciousness, the science of describing what one perceives, senses, and knows in one's immediate awareness and experience" (p. 26). Phenomenological research aims to "explore and search for the essential, invariant structure (essence) or the central underlining meaning of the experiences that contain both the outward appearance and inward consciousness based on the memories, images and meaning" (Moustakas, 1994, p. 52) of the participants. This method attempts to explore and elucidate the hidden and complex facets of the phenomenon being studied. Since the lived experience of the person with the phenomenon is a key component of this inquiry, a phenomenological approach is suitable for a study on how people experience and perceive rap, given the power and depth of the music as well as the myriad effects music has on people.

Participants

Purposive sampling will be used in order to obtain maximum variance within the sample: Key informants (student organizations and student leaders) in a large Midwestern university will be told of the study. Key informants will be asked to provide contact information for fans of hip hop and rap music who might be willing to participate. Those who are identified will be contacted by phone and/or e-mail and informed about the study. Approximately eight individuals will be identified to participate in this study, with an equal number of men and women. Ethnic diversity will be sought with at least one participant from each of these groups: whites, Asian Americans, African Americans, and Latinos. On the day of the interviews, participants will once again be informed about the study and told that they have the right to withdraw at any time. The participants will be given $10 for their time, and written consent to participate in the study will be obtained.

Instrumentation

The following open-ended questions will guide the semistructured interview:

1. When did you first start listening to hip hop/rap music?
2. What was that experience like and what does hip hop mean to you (the impact it has made on you)?
3. Who were/are your favorite artists? Please describe.
4. What have you learned or gained from hip hop?

5. What is negative about hip hop, and how do you deal with the possible negativity of the music?

The length of the in-depth and semistructured interviews will range from 30 minutes to one and a half hours. The interviews will be conducted by the first author and will be audiotaped and transcribed verbatim.

In order for the study's findings to be verified, the transcriptions and report of the study will be reviewed by the participants. Each participant will be asked to analyze and provide feedback on the significant statements, core themes, essence, and conclusions of the study. It is anticipated that some of the participants will provide comments and suggestions that will enhance the accuracy of the study, and their feedback will be integrated into the final report.

The following demographic information will be gathered: age, ethnicity, gender, level of education, family's socioeconomic status, type of community the participant grew up in, and participants' degree of academic success.

Phenomenological Inquiry Assumptions

Epoche, or bracketing, is a crucial component of phenomenological research. Epoche is defined as "the elimination of suppositions and raising of knowledge above every possible doubt" (Moustakas, 1994, p. 26). In this process, the researcher attempts to set aside his or her preconceived notions, assumptions, and knowledge of the experience or phenomenon under consideration in order to optimally grasp and freshly comprehend the participants' experiences with the phenomenon (Moerer-Urdahl & Creswell, 2004).

The lead researcher's experience of and interest in exploring the effects of rap music stem from his personal and extensive exposure to rap music. He is a fourth-generation Japanese American who grew up in a predominantly liberal middle-class white community in northern California. His first experience with rap music was when he was 10 years old. He enjoyed listening to cool beats and the amusing lyrics of DJ Jazzy Jeff and The Fresh Prince (Will Smith). When he attended junior high school, he had his first experience with explicit racism (being called names, picked on, and teased). During that time, he purchased Public Enemy's album in which the lyrics of the song "Shut 'Em Down" struck a chord and changed him forever. Identifying with the lyrics, he felt empowered and aware of the collective influence of race relations, oppression, and white power on his life. He felt understood and supported by groups such as Public Enemy and artists like Tupac Shakur and Notorious B.I.G. The rappers and their groups brought into focus the disenfranchisement of inner-city African Americans. This inspired him to become an advocate for disenfranchised groups. Years later, as an undergraduate, he began to analyze the lyrics and to discuss rap and hip hop with his friends. These were passionate conversations that inspired him to write an undergraduate paper on Tupac Shakur, which later was published in the *Black Scholar* (Iwamoto, 2003). Currently, he is in a counseling psychology doctoral program, and he also occasionally conducts hip hop analyses at community nonprofit programs.

Data Analysis

The first step in analyzing the phenomenological data will be to find and list significant statements—the process of *horizonalization*—that reflect participants' experience with rap music. Duplicate statements will be deleted, and the balance will be presented in a table.

After the significant statements have been reread and reflected upon, the Van Kaam method (Moustakas, 1994) will be used to determine if the statements can be categorized. In addition, we will look for statements that contain crucial elements of the experience that are applicable to understanding how rap music was experienced. The statements will be grouped into *clusters of themes and meaning units*. These will be presented in a second table.

The procedure after the themes have been clustered will be to devise the *structural and textual descriptions*. The structural description highlights the context and setting of the phenomenon.

Coinciding with this notion is the textual description—how the phenomenon was experienced and the description of the meaning the individual attributes to the experience (Moustakas, 1994).

The final step in phenomenological analysis is to amalgamate the structural and textural descriptions into one that captures the essence and meaning of the experience. The synthesis and description of the essence provides a holistic perspective about the phenomenon, though the "essences are never totally exhausted" (Moustakas, 1994, p. 100). The exhaustive description of the essence and meaning of rap music for ethnically diverse college students will be presented in a third table. In addition, a model of the essence of rap music will be constructed.

Discussion

This study will be one of the first qualitative studies to deeply explore how rap fans experience this music. Prior studies have been quantitative in nature and attempted to examine the effects of exposure to rap and how it relates to certain unhealthful behaviors. Other studies have been quasi-experimental and have addressed how hip hop can be implemented in prevention programs and group counseling. This study will focus on college students (Latinos, Asian Americans, and whites) and how they experience this music.

Consistency with Results of Previous Studies

We will consider whether the results of this study are consistent with Rubin et al.'s (2001) findings that rap music appeared to cultivate a greater sense of pride and self-concept. We will also consider whether our results are congruent with those of Arnett (1991), who found that despite heavy metal music having aggressive and violent messages, listeners reported feeling less anxious and stressed when listening to this type of music.

Implications

In light of the results of this study, the utility of rap music for use in college counseling will be considered. Since many adolescents are often reluctant or unwilling to participate in individual or group counseling, having a more comfortable topic to talk about, such as rap and hip hop music, might motivate participants to be more engaged in the counseling process. The results of this study may help counselors to better understand how to do this.

Similarly, rap music might be utilized in the education field. The results of this study may indicate how rap music as well as rap videos—if selected appropriately and facilitated by someone knowledgeable in these areas—can be an effective educational tool.

Limitations and Recommendations

The validity of the proposed study will be limited by the sampling procedure and the small number of participants. Even though various ethnic groups will be selected, the cases obviously will not be representative given the variations between and within ethnic and racial groups. Also, given that the participants will be purposefully drawn—knowledgeable fans of hip hop and rap music—it could be argued that they will represent a biased sample. Although the study will contain a small number of participants, it is worth noting that the number is within the sampling range for phenomenological studies (Creswell, 1998).

This study will contribute to the growing body of literature that addresses the potential counseling and educational implications of rap music for adolescents from diverse groups. Future studies might explore how other ethnic groups experience rap music (e.g., Native Americans, Arab Americans), as well as examine this subject quantitatively. Research in this area has barely skimmed the surface and, given rap's constant evolution, the research potential is limitless. Research in this area will continue to be relevant as youth worldwide continue to feel the beat of rap music.

References

Arnett, J. J. (1991). Adolescents and heavy metal music: From the mouths of metalheads. *Youth and Society*, *23*(63), 76–98.

Billboard Records. (2003, 2004). http://www.billboard.com.

Creswell, J. W. (1998). *Qualitative inquiry and research design: Choosing among five traditions*. Thousand Oaks, CA: Sage.

Iwamoto, D. K. (2003). Tupac Shakur: Understanding the identity formation of hyper-masculinity of a popular hip hop artist. *Black Scholar*, *33*(22), 44–49.

Miranda, D., & Claes, M. (2004). Rap music genres and deviant behaviors in French-Canadian adolescents. *Journal of Youth and Adolescence*, *33*(2), 113–122.

Moerer-Urdahl, T., & Creswell, J. (2004). Using transcendental phenomenology to explore the "ripple effect" in a leadership mentoring program. *International Journal of Qualitative Methods*, *3*(2). Article 2. Retrieved from: http://www.ualberta.ca/~iiqm/backissues/3_2/html/moerercreswell.html

Moustakas, C. (1994). *Phenomenological research methods*. Thousand Oaks, CA: Sage.

Richardson, J., & Scott, K. (2002). Rap music and its violent progeny: America's culture of violence in context. *Journal of Negro Education*, *71*(3), 175–192.

Rubin, A., West, D., & Mitchell, W. (2001). Differences in aggression, attitudes toward women, and distrust as reflected in popular music preferences. *Media Psychology*, *3*, 25–42.

Stephens, T., Braithwaite, R., & Taylor, S. (1998). Model for using hip hop music for small group HIV/AIDS-prevention counseling with African American adolescents and young adults. *Patient Education and Counseling*, *35*, 127–137.

Sullivan, R. (2003). Rap and race: It's got a nice beat, but what about the message? *Journal of Black Studies*, *33*(5), 605–622.

Tyson, E. (2002). Hip hop therapy: An exploratory study of a rap music intervention with at-risk and delinquent youth. *Journal of Poetry Therapy*, *15*(3), 131–144.

Wingood, G., DiClemente, R., Bernhardt, J., Harrington, K., Davies, S., Robillard, A., & Hook, E. (2003). A prospective study of exposure to rap music videos and African American female adolescents' health. *American Journal of Public Health*, *93*(3), 437–441.

Model Proposal 9: Combined Qualitative and Quantitative Research

Intimate Partner Abuse Perpetrated by Employees[1]

A Research Proposal Based on the Work of

Emily F. Rothman   Melissa J. Perry

Between 1992 and 1998, a total of 210 workers in the United States were killed on the job by an intimate partner, and it is estimated that roughly 18,700 nonfatal assaults by intimate partners are perpetrated in the workplace every year (Duhart, 2001; Sygnatur & Toscano, 2000). Given that roughly 25% of women and 8% of men in the United States experience intimate partner violence during their lifetimes, the frequency of these assaults in the workplace is not unexpected (Tjaden & Thoennes, 2000).

Since the mid-1990s, the U.S. business community has concerned itself with the social, criminal, and public health problems presented by partner violence. Largely, the corporate response to intimate partner violence has focused on victims. Policies designed to protect victims' confidentiality, assist them, or ensure their safety in the workplace have been developed, and in two cases evaluated with positive results (Issac, 1997; Urban & Bennett, 1999).

There are several reasons why companies are motivated to address the issue of partner violence experienced by their employees. Intimate partner violence victimization of women costs U.S. businesses an estimated $727.8 million each year in lost productivity, and, increasingly, senior management is becoming aware of the loss (National Center for Injury Prevention and Control, 2003). During a recent survey of Fortune 1,000 senior executives, 41% indicated that they believe domestic violence substantially affects profits (RoperASW, 2002). The proportion of these executives who say that they are personally aware of employees in their organizations who have been victims of domestic violence has increased by 16 percentage points during the past 8 years, from 40% in 1994 to 56% in 2002 (RoperASW, 2002). It is not surprising, then, that the number of corporate members of national groups such as the Corporate Alliance to End Partner Violence has increased dramatically in recent years (K. Wells, personal communication, April 21, 2003).

The proportion of U.S. workers who abuse intimates and the proportion of U.S. businesses that employ abusive workers are unknown. The cost of employing batterers remains similarly uninvestigated. However, both the humanistic and the profit concerns of employing *victims* of violence have generated significant involvement in violence prevention among corporate leaders such as American Express, CIGNA, Verizon Communications, Kraft Foods, Mary Kay Inc., State Farm Insurance Companies, and others (Corporate Alliance to End Partner Violence, 2002). In-

---

[1] This proposal was adapted from a report of completed research by Rothman, E. F., & Perry, M. J. (2004). Intimate partner abuse perpetrated by employees. *Journal of Occupational Health Psychology, 9,* 238–246. Copyright © 2004 by The Educational Publishing Foundation. Reprinted with permission. Correspondence about the completed research may be addressed to Emily F. Rothman, Boston University School of Public Health, 715 Albany Street, T253W, Boston, MA 02118. Electronic mail may be sent to EmFaith@aol.com. The affiliations of the authors are: Emily F. Rothman, Boston University School of Public Health, Department of Social and Behavioral Sciences; and Melissa J. Perry, Harvard School of Public Health, Department of Environmental Health.

vestigating and subsequently informing the business community about *perpetrators* of intimate partner violence would enhance existing efforts. Because many organizations have already begun the process of drafting domestic violence policies and victimization prevention programs, the added cost of extending existing policies, protocols, or assistance programming to those who abuse will be minimal. Additionally, the potential benefit of providing abusers with rehabilitative resources may have other indirect effects. It has been suggested that family violence perpetrators and perpetrators of workplace aggression may share some risk factors for abuse (Barling, 1996). Although the overlap between the two types of aggressors is unknown, it is possible that a reduction in workplace aggression may be observed in companies in which domestic safety becomes a focus.

From a liability perspective, experts disagree about employers' responsibility to intervene with employees who perpetrate violence that generally occurs off-site. Some question whether employers have a right to take action against employees for criminal behavior during nonworking hours and point out the legal constraints on conducting criminal background checks on job candidates (Bush & O'Shea, 1996). Counterbalancing these concerns is the fact that employers have been held liable in cases in which they retain batterers who reoffend (Johnson & Gardner, 1999), and that employers conceivably could be found liable if they fail to warn authorities when they have prior knowledge about the commission of a crime.

In the absence of existing literature on this topic, we will conduct a small-scale, exploratory study to generate hypotheses about batterers in the workplace for future investigation. Specifically, the four primary research questions of this study will be as follows: (a) Does perpetrating partner abuse affect employee productivity? (b) In what ways might employees who batter use workplace resources to perpetuate abuse? (c) How might employers respond to employees who are convicted of intimate partner abuse? (d) Which workplace policies and interventions might be effective at inhibiting abuse perpetration?

Method

Participants

The sample of participants will include approximately 30 employed men attending Massachusetts certified batterer intervention programs as the result of a criminal offense involving the abuse of an intimate partner. Participants will attend weekly batterer intervention counseling groups on a nonvoluntary basis for 8 to 38 weeks. Demographically, the participants who will be selected will be similar in age and race to the typical clients in Massachusetts certified batterer intervention programs (Massachusetts Department of Public Health, 2002). In addition, information on their occupations will be collected.

Data Collection and Response Rate

The qualitative data that are the primary focus of this study will be collected through four focus groups that will share an identical semistructured format based on a discussion guide. Supplementary quantitative data will be collected through a short survey that will be distributed at the beginning of each focus group. Focus group methods offer several advantages for the purpose of this investigation, including the promotion of self-disclosure around sensitive topics (Deane & Degner, 1997), enhancing the validity of data collected (Cirgin Ellett & Beausang, 2001), the opportunity to repeat and refine questions aloud for respondents who may have low literacy levels, and cost-effectiveness.

Four Massachusetts certified batterer intervention programs will be selected as recruitment sites out of 22 possible programs, on the basis of their geographic diversity and the ethnic diversity of their clients. Participants in the four focus groups will be recruited through flyers distributed by program counselors during batterer intervention group sessions. One week of free counseling at the respective batterer intervention programs (a value of $10–$25) will be advertised as compensation in exchange for participation in the focus groups. About 85 batterer intervention clients will be given the recruiting materials by program counselors, and it is anticipated that about one-third of them will choose to participate. Informed consent will be obtained from each participant.

Each focus group will be conducted in English, last approximately 2 hr, and will be audiotaped. The audiotapes will be transcribed.

Instruments

The 21-item quantitative survey will collect demographic information, the number of jobs held in the past 5 years, current occupation, termination history, and the perceived impact of intimate partner abuse perpetration on employment history. These questions will be presented in multiple-choice format, with the exception of one, which will require a write-in response. Two additional sets of questions on the quantitative survey will ask whether participants have used workplace resources to abuse victims (7 questions) or missed work time as a result of intimate partner abuse perpetration (5 questions). These questions will be presented in the form of checklists. Participants will be instructed to endorse the behaviors in which they have ever engaged. Face and construct validity of the question sets will be judged by a panel of seven experts that will include partner violence specialists and human resource professionals. The qualitative data will be collected through a discussion guide composed of open-ended questions. Sample questions for the qualitative data collection include: "How has your abusive behavior affected your time at work?" and "What, if anything, could an employer do to prevent batterers from abusing their partners?"

Analytic Strategy

Means and frequencies will be calculated from the quantitative survey data. The qualitative data will be analyzed in four phases by two independent raters, which is a standard approach to organizing and interpreting focus group data (Morgan, 1997). These four phases will be operationalized as follows: (a) Each of the four focus group transcripts will be read to give a "sense of the whole" (Feldman, 1994), (b) chunks of text will be identified and coded into a limited number of primary categories that reflect the research questions of interest, (c) coded chunks of text will be further subcoded for finer detail, and (d) the interrater agreement will be calculated and coding discrepancies will be resolved through consensus. According to Miles and Huberman (1994), a "chunk of text" may be a word, clause, sentence, or paragraph. For the purposes of this analysis, chunks are defined as words, sentences, or interchanges between focus group members that provide information about one of the four research questions of interest pertaining to (a) worker productivity, (b) using workplace resources to harm victims, (c) employers' response to employees who batter, and (d) workplace interventions with employees who batter.

The intercoder reliability relative to the four primary codes will be calculated according to the formula suggested by Miles and Huberman (1994): number of agreements divided by the total of the number of agreements plus the number of disagreements, resulting in a percentage of agreement for each of the four focus groups.

Discussion

On the basis of the results from this formative investigation, it should be possible to generate specific hypotheses about employees who batter.

There are several limitations to this proposed exploratory study. Perhaps the most important is that the comments made by the participants who volunteer to participate in the focus groups cannot be generalized to all batterers. Whether men who are convicted of partner abuse, are adjudicated to attend intervention programs, and volunteer to participate in focus group research are representative of batterers overall is unknown but unlikely. In addition, while the proposed sample size is adequate for the purposes of formative, qualitative research, it is insufficient for hypothesis testing or making inferences about the effect of batterers on their workplace in quantifiable terms. Large-scale empirical studies that test hypotheses resulting from the data generated by this proposed study will benefit the field.

Another potential threat to the validity of these data is the bias introduced through self-report, despite the fact it has been suggested that the homogeneity of focus groups encourage self-disclosure of sensitive topics (Deane & Degner, 1997). While it is possible that the participants in the study will minimize their own abusive behaviors or recall their employers' actions through a self-serving filter, neither of these biases will detract from what the participants do choose to reveal. A follow-up study that pairs batterers with employers and that surveys both groups for validation purposes would be of benefit. Similarly, a follow-up study that uses a comparison group of nonbatterers would provide additional insight as to whether batterers are any less productive than workers in general or workers with other criminal convictions.

In conclusion, employers face a dilemma when it comes to addressing partner abuse perpetrated by employees. If this study as well as forthcoming ones establishes that abusers do in fact reduce workplace productivity, increase costs to employers, create liability risks for employers, or are more likely than nonabusive counterparts to become violent with coworkers or managers, employers will feel pressure to respond with effective policies and training. On the other hand, if zero-tolerance policies create dangers for victims, or if employers are legally bound to respond to abusive employees in a manner they find disagreeable, or if the cost-benefit of intervention is not immediately felt, employers may decide that they are better off not getting involved. It is our hope that this dilemma will not deter employers from taking an interest in the issue of employees who batter but will serve as a call for larger, empirical testing of the hypotheses that will be developed as a result of this study. Ultimately, we hope that employers will eventually have a range of options for responding to intimate partner violence in a manner that is feasible, cost-effective, and successful at preventing further incidents.

References

Barling, J. (1996). Prediction, experience, and consequences of violence. In G. R. VandenBos & E. Q. Bulatao (Eds.), *Violence on the job* (pp. 29–50). Washington, DC: American Psychological Association.

Bush, D. F., & O'Shea, P. G. (1996). Workplace violence: Comparative use of prevention practices and policies. In G. R. VandenBos & E. Q. Bulatao (Eds.), *Violence on the job* (pp. 29–50). Washington, DC: American Psychological Association.

Cirgin Ellett, M. L., & Beausang, C. G. (2001). Introduction to qualitative research. *Gastroenterology Nursing, 25,* 10–14.

Corporate Alliance to End Partner Violence. (2002, Summer). *Newsletter, 7.*

Deane, K. A., & Degner, L. F. (1997). Determining the information needs of women after breast biopsy procedures. *AORN Journal, 65,* 767–776.

Duhart, D. T. (2001). *Violence in the workplace, 1993–99* (Bureau of Justice Statistics Special Report No. NCJ 190076). Washington, DC: U.S. Department of Justice, Office of Justice Programs.

Feldman, M. S. (1994). *Strategies for interpreting qualitative data.* Thousand Oaks, CA: Sage.

Issac, N. E. (1997). *Corporate sector response to domestic violence.* Boston: Harvard Injury Control Center.

Johnson, P. R., & Gardner, S. (1999). Domestic violence and the workplace: Developing a company response. *Journal of Management Development, 18,* 590–597.

Massachusetts Department of Public Health (2002). *Annual statistics of certified batterer intervention programs, 2001.* Boston: Massachusetts Department of Public Health, Department of Violence Prevention and Intervention Program Services.

Miles, M. B., & Huberman, A. M. (1994). *Qualitative data analysis.* Thousand Oaks, CA: Sage.

Morgan, D. L. (1997). *Focus groups as qualitative research.* Thousand Oaks, CA: Sage.

National Center for Injury Prevention and Control (2003). *Costs of intimate partner violence against women in the United States.* Atlanta: Centers for Disease Control and Prevention.

RoperASW (2002). *Corporate leaders on domestic violence: Awareness of the problem, how it's affecting their business, and what they're doing to address it.* New York: RoperASW.

Sygnatur, E., & Toscano, G. (2000, Spring). Work-related homicides: The facts. *Compensation and Working Conditions,* 3–8.

Tjaden, P., & Thoennes, N. (2000). *Prevalence, incidence, and consequences of violence against women: Findings from the National Violence Against Women Survey* (Report No. NCJ 183781). Washington, DC: U.S. Department of Justice.

Urban, B. Y., & Bennett, L. W. (1999). When the community punches a time clock: Evaluating a collaborative workplace domestic abuse prevention program. *Violence Against Women, 5*, 1178–1193.

Notes

Table 1

Table of Recommended Sample Sizes (n) for Populations (N) with Finite Sizes[1]

N	n	N	n	N	n
10	10	220	140	1,200	291
15	14	230	144	1,300	297
20	19	240	148	1,400	302
25	24	250	152	1,500	306
30	28	260	155	1,600	310
35	32	270	159	1,700	313
40	36	280	162	1,800	317
45	40	290	165	1,900	320
50	44	300	169	2,000	322
55	48	320	175	2,200	327
60	52	340	181	2,400	331
65	56	360	186	2,600	335
70	59	380	191	2,800	338
75	63	400	196	3,000	341
80	66	420	201	3,500	346
85	70	440	205	4,000	351
90	73	460	210	4,500	354
95	76	480	214	5,000	357
100	80	500	217	6,000	361
110	86	550	226	7,000	364
120	92	600	234	8,000	367
130	97	650	242	9,000	368
140	103	700	248	10,000	370
150	108	750	254	15,000	375
160	113	800	260	20,000	377
170	118	850	265	30,000	379
180	123	900	269	40,000	380
190	127	950	274	50,000	381
200	132	1,000	278	75,000	382
210	136	1,100	285	100,000	384

[1] Adapted from: Krejcie, R. V., & Morgan, D. W. (1970). Determining sample size for research activities. *Educational and Psychological Measurement, 30,* 607–610.

Notes

Appendix A

Locating Literature Electronically[1]

Increasingly, students are being given direct access to electronic databases in academic libraries. In this section, we will consider how to use them to locate articles in academic journals.

We will explore some of the important principles for locating literature electronically (via computer) from three major sources: (1) *Sociofile*, which contains the print versions of *Sociological Abstracts* and *Social Planning Policy & Development Abstracts*, covering journal articles published in more than 1,600 journals; (2) *PsycLIT*, which contains the print version of *Psychological Abstracts*, with abstracts to journal articles worldwide since 1974;[2] and (3) *ERIC*, which contains abstracts to articles in education found in more than 600 journals from 1966 to date.[3] The following characteristics are true of all three databases.

First, for each journal article, there is a single *record*; a record contains all the information about a given article. Within each record, there are separate *fields* such as the title field, the author field, the abstract (that is, summary of the article) field, and the descriptor field.

A descriptor is a key subject-matter term; for example, *learning environments*, *learning disabilities*, and *learning theories* are descriptors in *ERIC*. One of the important ways to access the databases is to search for articles using appropriate descriptors. Each database has a *thesaurus* with a list of available descriptors. It is important to refer to it to identify the terms you want to use in your search. For example, if your topic is *group therapy for child molesters*, the appropriate descriptors in *PsycLIT* are *group psychotherapy* and *pedophilia*.

Following are some principles for conducting a search. First, we can search a particular field or search entire records. If you have identified appropriate descriptors in the *thesaurus*, it is usually sufficient to search the descriptors field using the descriptors.[4]

---

[1] Patten, M. L. (2009). *Understanding research methods: An overview of the essentials* (7th ed.). Los Angeles: Pyrczak Publishing. Copyright © 2009 by Pyrczak Publishing. All rights reserved. Reprinted with permission.

[2] Use the print version for journal articles published before 1974.

[3] The emphasis in this appendix is on journal articles. Note that *PsycLIT* also abstracts books, *Sociofile* also abstracts dissertations, and *ERIC* also abstracts unpublished documents such as convention papers, which are available on microfiche.

[4] If you are not able to find appropriate descriptors, conduct a "free text" search using your own terms (such as *child molester*, which is not a *thesaurus* term) and searching entire records. If this term appears in any

We may conduct a search for all articles containing either (or both) of two descriptors by using OR. For example, the instruction to find *"dyslexia"* OR *"learning disabilities"* will locate all articles with either one of these descriptors. Thus, using OR broadens our search.

We can also broaden our search by using a root word such as *alcohol* followed by an asterisk (*); the asterisk instructs the program to search for the plural form as well as derivatives such as *alcoholism* and *alcoholics.*

Frequently, we wish to narrow our search in order to make it more precise. An important instruction for doing this is AND. For instance, if we use the instruction to locate articles with *"learning environments* AND *dyslexia,"* the program will only identify articles with *both* these descriptors and will exclude articles that have only one of them.

We can also make our search more precise by using NOT. The instruction *"advertising* NOT *television"* will identify all articles relating to advertising but exclude any that relate to advertising on television.

If you are working in a field with thousands of references, you can be more precise by adding another search concept such as age group (child, adolescent, adult, or elderly) and population (human or animal).

If you are required to use only recent references, you can also limit the search to recent years.

---

field in any of the records, the record(s) will be selected. If any are selected, examine the descriptors field to see what descriptors have been assigned to it; noticing *pedophilia*, you could now search again looking only in the descriptors field for the *thesaurus* descriptor, *pedophilia.*

Appendix B

Electronic Sources of Statistical Information[1]

When writing literature reviews, writers need up-to-date information. Because of the ease of electronic publishing, the Web usually has more up-to-date information than conventionally printed materials. (Note that it is not uncommon for a journal article or book to be published a year after it was written.)

It is often a good idea to begin literature reviews with current statistics on how many people (and/or the percentage of people) have a certain characteristic or a particular problem. Suppose, for instance, that your general topic for a literature review is cigarette smoking by pregnant women. Examine Box A, which shows two possible first sentences for a review. The second one, which cites current statistics found on the Web, is stronger and more compelling than the first one.[2]

Box A
The beginning of two possible first paragraphs for a literature review. The second one cites recent statistics found on the Web.

> 1. Many pregnant women continue to smoke despite warnings from the medical community. This makes it important to review literature to identify effective programs that....
>
> 2. Approximately 17% of pregnant women smoked cigarettes within the past month, according to a recent national survey (NHSDA, 1999).[3] This makes it important to review literature to identify... effective programs that....

Even if you do not begin your literature review with statistics, including specific statistics (e.g., "5,421 students" and "55.6% of the students") at some point in your literature review will make it more convincing than a review in which only vague references to statistics are made (e.g., "many individuals" and "a majority").

---

[1] This appendix was adapted from Chapter 4 (pp. 44–50) of Pan, M. L. (2004). *Preparing Literature Reviews: Qualitative and Quantitative Approaches* (2nd ed.). Los Angeles, CA: Pyrczak Publishing.
[2] Using simple, compelling statistics is appropriate in both qualitative and quantitative reviews.
[3] Retrieved at http://www.samhsa.gov/oas/2k2/PregAlcTob/PregAlcTob.html on September 19, 2002.

Note that many sources on the Web post the latest available information, which may not be completely up-to-date. For instance, the information in Box A was the most current available (for 1999) when retrieved in 2002. Nevertheless, a journal article or book published in 1999 would probably contain even older statistics given the publication lag in conventional, hard-copy publishing.

Note that Web addresses (i.e., URLs) frequently change, Web sites are often discontinued, and access that might be free at the time of this writing might not be free by the time you try to access them. If you have difficulties locating Web sites given in this book, use a general search engine such as www.Google.com to locate newer sites, additional free sites, and so on.

✎ Guideline 1   FedStats.gov is one of the most valuable sources of statistical information on the Web.

At www.FedStats.gov, you will be able to access statistics from more than 100 federal agencies.[4] Prior to the establishment of this Web site, writers needed to search for statistics agency by agency. While the FedStats site still allows you to search within only selected agencies, you can also search by *topic*, and the FedStats search engine will automatically search all agencies for relevant links to federal statistics. This is important for two reasons: (1) you do not have to search each agency separately, and (2) an agency that you are not aware of (or did not think of) may have statistics relevant to your topic.

For example, a topic search conducted by first going to www.FedStats.gov and clicking on Topic links – A to Z produced a screen with a row of letters of the alphabet underlined, followed by a list of categories for each letter. (As you know, Web links to other sites are usually underlined and/or are sometimes identifiable by other means such as the use of a different color for a link.) Clicking on the letter C in the row of letters produced the extensive set of links shown in Box B (on the next page). Clicking on the Breast link (the second link from the top) produced the links in Box C (on the following page).

---

[4] Be sure to go to www.FedStats.*gov* and *not* www.FedStats.*com*. The latter is *not* a government site. Also, be sure to type www. Although it is possible to access many sites on the Web without the prefix "www," this site is not one of them.

Box B

FedStats links for the letter "C."

Cancer:
-- *Atlas of Cancer Mortality in the United States*
-- Breast
-- Cervical
-- Lung
-- Mortality maps
-- Prostate
Charitable trusts
Children:
-- Administration for Children programs and services
-- Adoption
-- Aid to Families with Dependent Children
-- *America's Children* (ChildStats)
-- Behavior and social environment indicators
-- Child care
-- Child support enforcement
-- Cigarette smoking
-- Delinquency and victimization
   -- Delinquency case records
   -- Juvenile arrests
   -- Juveniles as offenders
   -- Juveniles as victims
   -- Juveniles in court
   -- Juveniles in detention and corrections
-- Drug use
-- Economic security indicators
-- Education indicators
-- Foster care
-- HeadStart
Health:
-- Child and infant
-- Indicators
-- Insurance
-- Population and family characteristics
-- Nutrition
-- WIC
Civil justice statistics
Coal
Commodity flow
Common cold
Communications:
-- Broadcast radio and television
-- Cable television providers by community served
-- Telephone industry and telephone usage
-- Wireless communications services
Computer and Internet use
Construction
Industry tax statistics:
-- Corporations
-- Exempt organizations' unrelated business
-- Partnerships
-- Sole proprietorship

Consumer Credit
Consumer product safety
Consumer Price Indexes
Consumption, energy
Corporations
Country profiles
Crime (See also *Law enforcement*):
-- Characteristics of crime
-- Children
-- Crime in schools
-- Crimes reported to the police
-- Criminal offenders
-- Drugs
-- Firearms
-- Hate
-- Homicide
-- Prison inmates
-- Terrorism
-- Victims
-- Violent
Criminal justice:
-- Corrections
   -- Capital punishment
   -- Inmates
   -- Jails
   -- Prisons
   -- Probation and parole statistics
-- Courts and sentencing
   -- Court organization
   -- Criminal case processing
   -- Pretrial release and detention
   -- Sentencing
-- Criminal record systems
-- Employment and expenditure
-- Federal justice statistics
-- Indigent defense statistics
-- Law enforcement
   -- Campus law enforcement
   -- Federal law enforcement
   -- State and local law enforcement
-- Prosecution
Crops:
-- Crop progress and weather, weekly
-- Data by county
-- Data by state, historic
-- Field
-- Fruits and nuts
-- Vegetables

Box C

A large sample of the links obtained by clicking on <u>Breast</u>, which is the second link in Box B (under the main heading "Cancer").

<u>**Treatment**</u>
Information about treatment, including surgery, chemotherapy, radiation therapy, immunotherapy, and vaccine therapy
• <u>Breast Cancer Treatment</u>
[<u>patients</u>] [<u>health professionals</u>]
• <u>Male Breast Cancer Treatment</u>
[<u>patients</u>] [<u>health professionals</u>]
• <u>Breast Cancer and Pregnancy</u>
[<u>patients</u>] [<u>health professionals</u>]
• <u>More Information</u>

<u>**Prevention, Genetics, Causes**</u>
Information related to prevention, genetics, and risk factors
• <u>Breast Cancer Prevention</u>
[<u>patients</u>] [<u>health professionals</u>]
• <u>Genetics of Breast and Ovarian Cancer</u>
• <u>Postmenopausal Hormone Use</u>
• <u>Long Island Breast Cancer Study Project</u>
• <u>More Information</u>

<u>**Screening and Testing**</u>
Information about methods of cancer detection, including new imaging technologies, tumor markers, and biopsy procedures
• <u>Breast Cancer Screening</u>
[<u>patients</u>] [<u>health professionals</u>]
• <u>NCI Statement on Mammography Screening</u>
• <u>HHS Affirms Value of Mammography</u>
• <u>More Information</u>

<u>**Clinical Trials**</u>
Information on clinical trials and current news on trials and trial-related data
• <u>Breast Cancer Updates</u>
• <u>Search for Clinical Trials</u>

<u>**Cancer Literature**</u>
Resources available from the CANCER-LIT® database
• <u>Search CANCERLIT®</u>
• <u>CANCERLIT® Topic Searches: Breast Cancer</u>
• <u>CANCERLIT® Topic Searches: Cancer Genetics</u>

<u>**Related Information**</u>
Other information, including reports about NCI priorities for cancer research and initiatives
• <u>Breast Cancer Progress Review Group</u>

<u>**Statistics**</u>
Information related to cancer incidence, mortality, and survival
• <u>Probability of Breast Cancer in American Women</u>
• <u>Breast - U.S. Racial/Ethnic Cancer Patterns</u>
• <u>Data Sources</u>

✎ Guideline 2   State and local governments and their agencies (including state-supported universities) often post very current statistics on the Web.

While you can obtain information at the local level at FedStats, you can sometimes obtain more current statistical information from nonfederal governmental sources. This is true for two reasons: (1) the federal government collects data periodically, with years intervening in some cases, and (2) local agencies must report in a very timely manner to their superiors such as city councils and mayors. Example 1 shows the latest statistics on property crimes in Buffalo, New York, posted on FedStats at the time of this writing as well as the latest ones obtained by going directly to the City of Buffalo Web site.[5]

---

[5] Retrieved September 19, 2002, from www.city-buffalo.com/Files/1_2_1/Police/Crime%20Statistics.html.

Example 1

Table 1

Property-Crime Statistics for Buffalo, New York, from Federal and Local Sources

Year	FedStats Web site	City of Buffalo Web site
2001	not available	16,185
2000	not available	16,591
1999	17,436	17,436

✎ Guideline 3   Use the raw statistics from governmental agencies—not statistics filtered by politicians or others with special interests.

Government statistics are usually collected by civil service employees (not political appointees). While there may be errors in their work, there is no more reason to suspect them of deliberately biasing the data collection than to suspect any other type of researcher. However, some politicians may understandably be selective (and perhaps misleading) in choosing which statistics to report. Hence, it is usually best to obtain the original government reports either in print or via the Web rather than relying on second-hand reports of government statistics presented by politicians or special-interest groups and organizations. However, as you will see in Guideline 5, those with vested interests in statistical information sometimes provide useful links or primary-source information (via the Web), which can be helpful when writing literature reviews.

Note that in some cases, it is appropriate to present original government statistics in a literature review *and* discuss how they are interpreted by individuals and organizations with varying political points of view.

✎ Guideline 4   Consider consulting the Library of Congress's Virtual Reference Shelf on the Web.

The Library of Congress maintains a Web site titled the "Virtual Reference Shelf." It is an excellent site for general references such as dictionaries, general history, abbreviations, genealogy, and so on. The "Virtual Reference Shelf" can be accessed at www.loc.gov/rr/askalib/virtualref.html.[6] Box D shows the main links at that site. Although these links take you to a wide variety of types of information, they often include statistics on various topics. At the bottom of the home page (not shown in the box but clearly visible on the Web site) is a link for "Ask a Librarian," which can be a very useful

---

[6] Rather than typing (and risk mistyping) long URLs, it is sometimes faster to conduct a quick search on a major search engine such as www.Google.com using a term such as "Virtual Reference Shelf." Use quotation marks around the terms (e.g., "Virtual Reference Shelf") to conduct an exact phrase match and exclude other Web sites that might have only one of the words, such as "virtual."

service if you are struggling to find specialized statistical information to use in your literature review.

Box D

Links on the home page of the Library of Congress's Virtual Reference Shelf.

Internet Public Library Reference Center
Librarian's Index to the Internet Refdesk

- Abbreviations
- Almanacs and Fast Facts
- Associations
- Awards/Prizes
- Books, Periodicals, and Publishing
- Business
- Calculators
- Clocks/Times
- Consumer Information
- Current Events on the Web
- Dictionaries/Thesauri
- Directories
- Domestic Arts

- Education
- Encyclopedias
- Genealogy, Biography, and Archaeology
- General History
- Health/Medical
- Language and Literature
- Law
- Libraries
- Maps/Driving Directions
- Political Science and Government
- Quotations
- Statistics
- Technology and Engineering (Weather)

Selected Subject Feature * Other Reference Sites * In the News

---

✎ **Guideline 5   Consider accessing information posted on the Web by a variety of nongovernmental agencies, such as businesses, professional associations, and advocacy groups.**

A wide variety of associations post information (and statistics) on the Web. Following the link called "Associations" in the Virtual Reference Shelf (see Box D), you can identify hundreds of associations, many of which are quite specialized. For instance, there are employee associations such as the Southern California Association of Fingerprint Officers at www.scafo.org, which publishes an online journal titled *The Print* in which there are original articles as well as reprints of articles from other sources. In contrast, there are political lobbying and advocacy associations such as the Web site for the American Civil Liberties Union at www.aclu.org, which publishes a newsletter and sells inexpensive special reports such as *Unequal, Unfair, and Irreversible: The Death Penalty in Virginia*, which cites relevant statistics.

Be cautious when citing information found on Web sites maintained by advocacy groups such as unions and political-interest groups. Nevertheless, because of their special interest in topics related to their missions, advocacy groups may have more information than other sources because they have sought it out more thoroughly than others have or because they have conducted their own unpublished studies. Note that you might want to compare and contrast the points of view of opposing advocacy groups in your literature review. For instance, you might point out how the Republican candidate for an office interprets a change in unemployment statistics and compare it with how the Democratic candidate interprets the same statistics. Note that while the statistics cited by politicians (and others) are secondary-source material, the *interpretations* of the statistics are primary sources of information.

You should also consider accessing information posted on the Web by businesses and corporations. Suppose you are writing a literature review on allergies for a health education class. Going to the home page for the prescription drug Flonase® will provide you with a reference to an article on allergies in an academic journal.

Keep in mind that complete objectivity in research cannot be achieved. All agencies sponsoring research (even nonprofit ones that have special tax status) have points of view that might influence what is researched, how questions are worded, how the sample is drawn, how the information is presented, and so on. It is your responsibility to try to understand their points of view and identify information on the Web that is reliable and useful for the purposes of your literature review.

Notes

Notes

Notes